First Step of
Credit Risk Management

...Exclusively SME

CA Ram Sarikh

Table of content

1 SME in India – An overview

Industry overview

SMEs are now exposed to greater opportunities than ever for expansion and diversification across the sectors. Indian market is growing rapidly and Indian entrepreneurs are making remarkable progress in various Industries like Manufacturing, Precision Engineering Design, Food Processing, Pharmaceutical, Textile & Garments, Retail, IT and ITES, Agro and Service sector.

Companies in India operate at very low scale of production and this hinders their ability to cater to the international markets Capturing a certain scale of operations is very critical in the SMEs growth path. Management depth an industry wide challenge but one that impacts SMEs in India the most is the lack of managerial depth. SMEs are driven largely by entrepreneurial spirit. The entrepreneur's core strength and customer relationships are key success factors that drive the business.

In 2010-11 budget allocation of Rs, 2400 crore for SMEs which has been raised from Rs. 1800 crore that is a substantial jump of about 33 per cent in one year.
The State-wise distribution of SMEs shows that more than 55% of these enterprises are in 6 States, namely, Uttar Pradesh, Maharashtra, Tamil Nadu, West Bengal, Andhra Pradesh and Karnataka. Further, about 7% of SMEs are owned by women.

According to a recent study by D&B, SMEs have a very strong presence in the Northern part of India followed by West and South. SMEs follow the automotive industry clusters of Gurgaon, Pune and Chennai. Data furnished by ACMA (Automotive Component Manufactures Association of India) showed an industry turnover of Rs.1, 821 crore (USD 39.9 billion) in 2010-11.

Banks are mandated to maintain 40% of their total credit outlay for priority-sector lending (i.e. agricultural, rural, SME and micro-lending).It is also interesting to note that within the 40% target, there are no minimum targets for the SSI/SME sector itself. most banks have now shifted to lending to MF s at not-so-competitive rates, who in turn, transfer some of the high interest costs to the end-borrowers.

Defining SMEs in India In accordance with the provision of Micro, Small & Medium Enterprises Development (MSMED) Act, 2006 the Micro, Small and Medium Enterprises (MSME) are classified in two classes:

Description	Manufacturing Enterprises Investment in Plant & Machinery	Services Enterprises Investment in Equipments
Micro Enterprises	Upto Rs. 25 Lakh	Upto Rs. 10 Lakh
Small Enterprises	Above Rs. 25 Lakh & Upto Rs. 5 Crores	Above Rs. 10 Lakh & Upto Rs. 2 Crores
Medium Enterprises	Above Rs. 5 Crores & Upto Rs. 10 Crores	Above Rs. 200 lakh & Upto Rs. 5 Crores

Sources: Data published by CRISIL

Contribution and Importance

Small and Medium Enterprises (SMEs) play a vital role for the growth of Indian economy as:
- There are approximately 30 million SME Units in India.
- Produce more than 8000 quality products for the Indian and international markets.
- It contributes 45% of industrial output.
- It contributes to 40% of exports of the country
- It is employing 60 million people and creating 1.3 million jobs every year. About 12 million persons are expected to join the workforce in the next 3 years.
- SME's Contribution towards GDP in 2011 was 17% which is expected to increase to 22% by 2012.

Region wise Penetration of SME's units in India

Geographical Distribution of SME's		
Zone	Units	Total
North Zone		
Punjab	9 %	
Uttar Pradesh	6%	
Haryana	5%	
Rajasthan	4%	
Himachal Pradesh	2%	
New Delhi	5%	
Chhattisgarh	1%	32%
West Zone		
Maharashtra	22%	
Gujarat	10%	32%
South Zone		
Tamil Nadu	10%	
Andhra Pradesh	8%	
Kerala	1%	
Orissa	3%	
Karnataka	5%	27%
East Zone		
West Bengal	4%	
Madhya Pradesh	3%	7%
Others	2%	2%
		100%

Sources: Data published by CRISIL

As per the data below, maximum SME's are in Manufacturing & constitution is partnership & proprietorship i.e. 54%

Nature of Business Operations	
Types of Business	Percentage
Manufacturing	83%
Services	9%
Trading	6%
Job work	2%
Total	100%

Constitution of Enterprises	
Private limited company	35%
Public limited company	9%
Partnership	24%
Proprietorship	30%
others	2%
Total	100%

Sources: Data published by CRISIL

Industry wise distribution

As per the data below, the maximum SME units are into Agri products and FMCG then Engineering products.

Industry wise Distribution	
Industry wise Distribution	Percentage concentration
Agri products and FMCG	10
Steel and Steel products	6
Auto Ancillary	4
Pharmaceuticals	3
Printing	3
Chemicals	3
Wood and wood products	2
Paper & Paper products	1
Hospital & health care	1
Gems, jewellery & watches	1
Engineering	8
Textile and Readymade	6
Plastic & Plastic products	4
Construction-Civil	3
Electric Equipments	3
Education	2
Casting/Fittings	1
IT and ITES	1
Rubber products	1
Others	34

Sources: Data published by CRISIL

Export Destinations

Export Destinations for SME's	
Countries	Percentage
EU	39%
USA	30%
Asia Pacific	12%
Middle East Asia	9%
Africa	6%
SAARC	4%
Total	100%

Potential export destinations for products of SMEs are the USA, EU and Japan.

Product group	Main destination (countries)	States producing these products
Readymade garments	USA, Europe, Canada, West Asia and North Africa	Punjab, Haryana, Tamil Nadu and Maharashtra
Plastic items	UAE, China, Italy, Saudi Arabia and Oman	Various
Marine products	Japan, USA, EU, China and South-East Asia.	Kerala, Tamil Nadu, West Bengal, Maharashtra and all the coastal states
Sports goods	UK, USA, Australia, Germany and South Africa	Punjab, Haryana, Tamil Nadu and Maharashtra
Spices	East Asia, EU, North African Zone and American Zone	Various
Cashew items	USA, Netherlands, UK, Japan and UAE	Maharashtra, Andhra Pradesh, Kerala and Orissa
Shellac items	Indonesia, Germany, UAE, USA and Italy	Various
Synthetic items (Madeups)	UAE, UK, Turkey, USA and Italy	Various
Leather and leather items	Germany, UK, Italy, USA and France	Uttar Pradesh
Engineering and electronic items	USA, Europe, Japan, Hong Kong, UAE, Germany, Belgium and France	Maharashtra, Tamil Nadu and Karnataka
Basic chemical and cosmetic products	USA, Japan, Saudi Arabia, China, Singapore and Netherlands	Various
Chemical and allied products	Japan, Belgium, Italy, France, Bangladesh, USA and UK	Various
Wool and woolen knitted garments	Europe, Japan, and Bangladesh	Punjab
Processed food items	USA, Europe and Japan	Various
Electronic items and computer software	USA, Hong Kong, UAE, UK,Germany, and Japan	Maharashtra, Karnataka, Andhra Pradesh, and Haryana
Tobacco and tobacco items	East Europe	Andhra Pradesh and Karnataka

Sources: Data published by CRISIL

SME Financing

- SME financing is a high risk funding for banks that's why banks are reluctant to take big exposure in SME's, generally they provide working capital to them or look for a collateral requirement such as property or guarantee.
- Unlike specific sectors, SME's do not maintain proper books and financials. Most of their business is in cash which makes it difficult in access their financial strength.
- In the absence of the next level of management the entrepreneur assumes multiple roles within the organization diluting the core focus of developing and driving company's growth avenues. This leads to larger issues of management vision and building sustainability of the business.
- The lack of collateral is probably the most widely cited obstacle encountered in financing SME's.
- The cost of funding is high in SME's. Cost of appraising a loan application—or of conducting a due diligence exercise in view of a possible equity investment—is largely independent from the size of the financing under consideration. In the case of smaller loans or investments, it is more difficult to recoup these costs.

Strength of SMEs

- The SME sector is often driven by individual creativity. A major strength of the sector is its potential for greater innovation both in terms of products and processes.
- An inherent strength of the sector is that these enterprises can be set up with very small amounts of investments and have the location flexibility to be located anywhere in the country.
- Their employment potential is higher as compared to large enterprises and are presently estimated to employ 60 million people.
- They are amenable to ancilliarisation and thus have natural linkages with large enterprises.
- They have short gestation period and have a lower administrative cost.
- Induce growth of industrially backward regions ensuring balanced regional development.

Weakness of SMEs

- Only 1.5 million are in the registered segment while the remaining 28.2 million (94%) are in the unregistered segment .There are 1. 38Lacs sick units within the sector.
- The sector is heterogeneous with pockets of high technology enterprises and majority suffering from low technology base resulting in low productivity and poor quality of product.
- The units being small in size also have poor access to credit and equity.
- While we have large pool of human resources, this sector continues to face shortage of skilled manpower due to lack of paying capacity and lack of poor managerial Capabilities.
- The absence of marketing channels and brand building equity is also one of the major weaknesses of this sector.

- There is a lack of coordination among the various organizations involved in the promotion of SMEs, including organizations of the State/UT Governments and poor linkages with the institutional stakeholders in the private sector.
- The absence of a suitable exit mechanism is a major constraint for the entrepreneurs.
- The lack of reliable and updated data base is another area of concern as it inhibits monitoring of development initiatives and formulation of appropriate schemes to meet.

Challenges

- Despite its commendable contribution to the Nation's economy, SME Sector does not get the required support from the concerned Government Departments, Banks, Financial Institutions and Corporate, which is a handicap in becoming more competitive in the National and International Markets.
- SMEs faces a number of problems - absence of adequate and timely finance and at cheaper rates, limited capital and knowledge, non-availability of suitable technology, low production capacity, ineffective marketing strategy and R&D, identification of new markets, constraints on modernisation & expansions, lack of proper management and accounting practices, non availability of highly skilled labour at affordable cost, follow-up with various government agencies to resolve problems etc.

Measure to promote the sector/Prospects

SMEs are the fountain head of several innovations in manufacturing and service sectors, the major link in the supply chain to corporate and the PSUs. By promoting SMEs, the rural areas of India will be developed.

- For raising funds, as BSE and NSE are racing to launch the SME Stock Exchanges to provide a trading platform for the SME sector.
- As per a report published by CRISIL in Jan 2011, which studies the funding patterns of 2000 small and medium enterprises (SMEs) in India. It reveals that there is scope for banks to increase their lending to SMEs by Rs.500 billion. The funding opportunity is greater for smaller SMEs where turnover is less than Rs.500 lakh. Furthermore, the study reveals that the urban areas have greater scope than their counterparts in the semi-urban and rural areas to increase funding support to SMEs.
- A quality certification scheme has been launched to improve the quality standards of the products which are to be assisted by awareness programmes and financial support to acquire ISO 9000 or similar international quality standards
- SIDBI introduced a scheme of assistance for supporting the development of industrial areas. Under the scheme, assistance will be extended to the state small industries development corporations state infrastructure development corporations and other such bodies engaged in developing industrial areas.
- Small enterprises are treated as a priority sector for extending credit by financing institutions. As such, 10 percent of the total credit to be advanced by commercial banks should go to small scale units.
- The NSIC has launched a B2B web portal and established a marketing intelligence cell which shall provide database and information support to the SMEs. It can therefore be seen that the government has adopted a multi-faceted program me of development for SMEs. This program I have gained strength with the adoption of the new policy for small industries.

Important Organization Associated with SME:

- Important organizations associated with small-scale industry are:
- Small Industries Development Organization (SIDO),
- Small Scale Industries Board (SSIB),
- National Small Industries Corporation Ltd. (NSIC),
- Confederation of Indian Industry (CII),
- Federation of Indian Chamber of Commerce and Industry (FICCI),
- PHD Chamber of Commerce and Industry (PHDCCI),
- Associated Chamber of Commerce and Industry of India (ASSOCHAM),
- Federation of Indian Exporters Organization(FIEO),
- World Association for Small and Medium Enterprises (WASME),
- Federation of Associations of Small Industries of India (FASII),
- Consortium of Women Entrepreneurs of India (CWEI),
- Laghu Udyog Bharti (LUB),
- Indian Council of Small Industries (ICSI),
- Indian Institute of Entrepreneurship (IIE),
- National Institute of Small-Industry Extension Training (NISIET),
- National Backward Caste Finance Development Corporation,
- National Institute for Entrepreneurship and Small Business Development (NIESBUD),
- Small Entrepreneurs Promotion and Training Institute (SEPTI),
- Small Industries Development Bank of India (SIDBI) etc.

2 Non Banking Finance Company- An RBI Perspective

According to the Economic Survey 2010-11, it has been reported that NBFCs as a whole account for 11.2 per cent of assets of the total financial system. With the growing importance assigned to financial inclusion, NBFCs have come to be regarded as important financial intermediaries particularly for the small-scale and retail sectors.

Meaning and Types of NBFCs:

Section 45I of the Reserve Bank of India Act, 1934 defines "non-banking financial company" as—

I. A financial institution which is a company;
II. A non-banking institution which is a company and which has as its principal
III. business of receiving deposits, under any scheme or arrangement or in any other manner, or lending in any manner;
IV. Such other non-banking institution or class of such institutions, as the Bank may, with the previous approval of the Central Government and by notification in the Official Gazette, specify.

NBFCs vs. Conventional Banks:

An NBFC cannot accept demand deposits, and therefore, cannot write a cheque facility.

I. It is not a part of payment and settlement system which is precisely the reason why it cannot issue cheques to its customers.
II. Deposit insurance facility of DICGC is not available for NBFC depositors unlike in case of banks.
III. **SARFAESI Act provisions have not currently been extended to NBFCs.**
IV. Besides the above, NBFCs pretty much do everything that banks do.

Classification of NBFCs

(1) Loan Company (LC)
Loan company means any company which is a financial institution carrying on as it's principal business the providing of finance whether by making loans or advances or otherwise for any activity other than its own but does not include an Asset Finance Company.

(2) Investment Company(IC)
Investment Company is a company which is a financial institution carrying on as it's principal business the acquisition of securities.

(3) Asset Finance Company (AFC)
AFC would be defined as any company which is a financial institution carrying on as its principal business the financing of physical assets supporting productive / economic activity, such as automobiles, tractors, lathe machines, generator sets, earth moving and material handling equipments, moving on own power and general purpose industrial machines.

Financing of physical assets may be by way of loans, lease or hire purchase transactions. Principal business for this purpose is defined as aggregate of financing real/physical assets supporting economic activity and income arising there from is not less than 60% of its total assets and total income respectively.

(4) Infrastructure Finance Company (IFC)

The above-mentioned types of NBFCs may be further classified into:

- NBFCs accepting public deposit (NBFCs-D) and
- NBFCs not accepting/holding public deposit (NBFCs-ND).

Further Classification of NBFCs-ND based on the Size of its Asset:

NBFCs-ND may also be classified into **(i)** Systematic Investment and **(ii)** Non- Systematic Investment NBFCs based on the size of its asset.

Systemically Important NBFCs-ND

An NBFC–ND with an asset size of Rs.100 crore and more as per the last audited balance Sheet is considered as systemically important NBFCs–ND (NBFC-ND-SI). However NBFCs–ND–SI are required to maintain a minimum CRAR of 10 per cent. No NBFC–ND–SI is allowed to:

- Lend to any single borrower/group of borrowers exceeding 15 per cent / 25 percent of its owned fund;
- Invest in the shares of another company/ single group of companies exceeding 15 per cent /25 per cent of its owned fund; and
- lend and invest (loans/investments taken together) exceeding 25 per cent of its owned fund to a single party and 40 per cent of its owned fund to a single group of parties.

Non-Systematically Important NBFCs-ND

A NBFC–ND whose asset size does not exceed Rs.100 crore as per the last audited balance sheet may be considered as Non-systemically important NBFCs–ND (NBFCND-SI).

Till March 2011 there were 12,739 NBFCs out of which 336 NBFCs were permitted to accept public deposits

Funding Source of NBFCs

Funding sources of NBFCs include debentures, borrowings from banks and FIs, Commercial Paper and inter-corporate loans.

NBFCs are typically into funding of:

- Personal Loan
- Construction equipment
- Commercial vehicles and cars
- Gold loans
- Microfinance
- Consumer durables and two wheelers
- Loan against shares
- Loan against property
- Machine & Equipment

Future prospects of NBFC sector:

NBFCs have been playing a very important role both from the macroeconomic perspective and the structure of the Indian financial system. NBFCs are the perfect or even better alternatives to the conventional Banks for meeting various financial requirements of a business enterprise. They offer quick and efficient services without making one to go through the complex rigmarole of conventional banking formalities. However to survive and to constantly grow, NBFCs have to focus on their core strengths while improving on weaknesses. They will have to be very dynamic and constantly endeavour to search for new products and services in order to survive in this ever competitive financial market.

Since NBFCs have been kept outside the purview of SARFAESI Act, a reform in this area is quite urgently needed. A suitable legislative amendment extending the operation of the said Act to NBFCs too would go a long way in fortifying the faith of the investors and which in turn would greatly contribute to the growth of this Sector. The coming years will be very crucial for NBFCs and only those who will be able to face the challenge and prove themselves by standing the test of time will survive in the long run.

3 Introduction to credit risk management

Lending has always been the primary function of banking, and accurately assessing a borrower's creditworthiness has always been the only method of lending successfully.
The method of analysis required varies from borrower to borrower. It also varies in function of the type of lending being considered.

For example, the banking risks in financing the building of a hotel or rail project, of providing lending secured by assets or a large overdraft for a retail customer would vary considerably.
For the financing of the project, you would look to the funds generated by future cash flows to repay the loan, for asset secured lending, you would look at the assets and for an overdraft facility, you would look at the way the account has been run over the past few years.
In this study material on credit risk management, we will be looking specifically at the appropriate methods of analysis for lending to companies, a subject more often known as 'corporate credit'.

What is the role of credit analyst?

Credit analysis supports the work of marketing officers by evaluating companies before lending money to them.
This is essential so that new loan requests can be processed, a company's repayment ability assessed, and existing relationships monitored.
The extent of the credit analysis is determined by

- The size and nature of the enquiry,
- The potential future business with the company,
- The availability of security to support loans,
- The existing relationship with the customer.

The analysis must also determine whether the information submitted is adequate for decision-making purposes, or if additional information is required.

An analysis can therefore cover a wide range of issues.

For example, in evaluating a loan proposal for a company, it may be necessary to:
- Obtain credit and trade references,
- Examine the borrower's financial condition,

Putting a provision in loan agreement appropriately for covering the risk.

Consult with legal counsel regarding a particular aspect of the draft loan agreement. By making these checks you are ensuring that your report does not look at a company's creditworthiness in a narrowly defined sense. You will be taking the further step of deciding whether the provisions in the loan agreement are appropriate for the borrower's financial condition.

Often it will be necessary for the analyst to place the assessment of the borrower's financial condition within the wider context of the conditions existing in the industry in which it is operating.

For example: Is the company's business seasonal or normal? How will this affect the long-term cash flow of the firm? What are the considerations of general economic conditions and, if appropriate, political conditions in the country where the company is operating?

Overview of credit analysis Process

Credit analysis includes financial and non-financial factors, and these factors are all interrelated. These factors include:

- The environment,
- The industry,
- Competitive position,
- Financial risks,
- Management risks,
- Loan structure and documentation issues.

ll companies operate in an economic and business environment, there- fore, when beginning to analyze a company, it is important to situate the company within this context.

Environment is important – whilst management cannot control the environment, it needs to function within it and therefore limit the impact of potentially adverse changes and ensure that it has resources to with- stand them.

We shall consider each of these factors in detail, starting with macro- economic factors which affect the economy and sectors of the industry and then focus on company risk and the risks that might affect particular loans.

Framework for credit Analysis:

A)   Types of Lending

i)   Unsecured Loan

ii)   Secured Loan

B)   Understanding of business model, product/Services, management & industry

C)   Understanding financial position of borrower

i)   Financial documents

ii)   Analytical methodology(i.e. CAT)

iii)   Problem with financial statements & auditors

D)   Outside information

E)   Transaction structure defined

A)   Types of lending

The starting point in analyzing the creditworthiness of a company is to consider the type of lending being proposed. It is important to establish this before analyzing the financial condition of the borrower because there are different risks involved in different types of lending.

Establishing what type of lending is being proposed will define the approach to be adopted in assessing the creditworthiness of a company. The three primary types of lending and their risks are as follows:

i)   Unsecured loan(Seasonal & Normal business)

ii)   Secured Loan

i)   Unsecured loan (Seasonal & Normal business)

Farming, package tour holidays, ski equipment, or sugar are typical seasonal businesses.

A banker dealing with a sugar industry would expect an increasing overdraft during is season as the company buys raw materials and builds up stock which is then processed into finished goods. The overdraft would be substantially reduced as the asset is sold, usually on credit.

Such short-term financing is repaid from the cash collected when the goods are paid for. This process is called the cash or asset conversion cycle.

The primary risk in this type of lending is the company's inability to complete the conversion of the asset into cash, due to failures in the supply, manufacturing, sales, or debt collection phase of the cycle.

The analyst should be concerned with the liquidity of the assets being financed (would they be easy to sell in a forced sale?) and management's ability to complete the asset conversion cycle.

Furthermore, the loan facility and documentation should be structured in such a manner so that the lender can monitor the borrower's condition frequently and retain control in lending funds or renewing the facility.

A.   Secured loan

This is lending to finance a company's medium to long-term needs (5–7 years typically) Often, the loan is to purchase an asset that is expected to generate future cash flow and contribute towards the repayment of the loan. The assets being financed by the facility. such as plant or equipment, are usually expected to produce other assets which, when converted to cash through completion of the manufacturing process and sale, will generate sufficient funds to repay the loan. The fixed asset itself is therefore not expected be converted to cash to repay the loan, which means that this type of loan is not self-liquidating. Rather, profits produced by the new equipment are the source of cash used to repay the loan. This process is expected to occur over the long, not short term.

Your primary concern in this type of lending is the company's ability to proper utilization of assets and to increase the future cash flows.

B) Understanding of business model, products, management & Industry

Analyst should develop the very good understanding about the business model of the borrower. He should first understand what is the source of business, its process, its marketing mechanism etc. Is the process very technical, or moderate, or it has required very heavy & costly machineries.

Analyst should develop understanding about its products/services. Is it in high demand or low demand. What is the USP of its products. What is the future of that product.

Analyst should also develop understanding about its management & organizational structure. Whether its current management is capable to handle all the activities. No of professionally qualified & technical personnel in whole management.

And most important what is the current scenario of industry in which it falls. What is the future prospect of that industry. E.g. textile industry maximum depends upon yarn prices. If it is very high than it will badly affects the whole textile industry.

C) Understanding of Financial Covenants of the borrower

In India, constitution of companies has been defined on the basis of:-

A) **Limited liability** – Pvt Ltd, Public Ltd, LLP
B) **Unlimited Liability**- Proprietorship, Partnership, HUF, AOP, BOI

For analyzing the financial health of the borrower analyst take majorly following documents according to the constitution of customer:
   a) Financial statements (i.e. B/S , P&L, CFS, Notes to accounts, Auditors report , Director report)
   b) Bank statements(including CC/OD sanction letter/repayment schedules)
   c) Tax Audit Report
   d) Income tax Returns
   e) Vat/Sales Tax/ Service tax return
   f) MOA/AOA/Partnership deed
   g) List of Directors & Shareholding pattern
   h) KYC documents

   (We will discuss in details all of above in financial Risk chapter)

Analytical methodology spreading the statements (Credit Appraisal Tool)

Account presentations vary considerably from country to country, company to company, and even from year to year. Company may present its financial statements in horizontal or vertical form. But as per schedule VI of company's act 1956, every company has to present its financial statements in vertical form only except banking, electricity & insurance companies. As they have other prescribed format under the act governing such class of company like banking regulation act, electricity act & insurance act.

Analysis is therefore easier when the company accounts are reclassified into a standardized format that avoids distortions and is familiar to the credit analyst. Such standardized formats enable comparison with competitors and industry sectors.

This standardized format is known as a 'spreadsheet or Credit Appraisal Tool (CAT) shows the assets and l abilities side of the balance sheet, income statement (with reconciliation of changes in retained earnings), and usually a ratio sheet incorporating a selection of financial ratios and a cash-flow model.

There is a range of industry specific spreadsheets for different companies including banks, insurance companies, finance houses, and manufacturers.

Spreadsheets are designed to present the company's financial details in a clear format which highlights key groupings of accounts and permits historical comparisons as well as comparisons with other companies. Most spreadsheets provide blank spaces for entering items peculiar to an individual concern or industry.

- The balance sheet spreadsheet format usually follows the standard arrangement in auditors' reports. Assets are arranged in descending order of fixed assets : fixed assets, investments, and other resources at the top, followed by current assets such as cash, marketable securities, debtors (accounts receivable), and stock (inventory). Liabilities are arranged long-term debt, subordinated debt, and equity at the top, followed by with short-term overdrafts and bank debt.

- The income statement spreadsheet is likewise based on the statement and provides the means for studying the underlying financial condition of the company. Major items are also shown as ratios or percent- ages to the net sales figure, since consideration of these relationships is necessary for a comprehensive analysis of operating efficiency. Following the net profit or net income figure the analyst must reconcile amounts paid out as dividends and amounts paid into reserves so that the retained earnings figure balances with the actual changes registered in the balance sheet.

- The Cash-Flow Reconciliation Statement is a statement incorporating elements from both the balance sheet and income statement spread- sheets. It is designed to highlight the movements in cash, on a cash basis (immediate) rather than accrual (based over time) basis. It enables one to see whether the company operated with a cash surplus or deficit and identify where the company's funds were utilized during the year.

Whilst spreading financial statements is tedious and time consuming, the bank as a lender needs to exercise due diligence in its lending activities. Lending decisions based on unaudited information provided by third parties leaves the bank in a vulnerable legal position; it is there- fore essential that the bank using such pre prepared financial statements understand how these spreadsheets are produced in order to be able to identify any potential anomalies.

Sample blank spreadsheet (CAT)

Here is an example of a summary balance sheet and P/L spreadsheet for a corporate. Such a 'blank' spreadsheet is typically used by bankers to recast company accounts into a legible format, typically for entities which are not large enough to be included in databases.

PARTICULARS	AUDITED		AUDITED		AUDITED
	31-Mar-11	% Growth	31-Mar-10	% Growth	31-Mar-09
PROFIT & LOSS ACCOUNT	Rs. Lacs	#N/A	Rs. Lacs	#N/A	Rs. Lacs
Sales/Receipts					
Other Income (part of Business Income)					
Other Income (Non Business income)					
TOTAL INCOME	0.0		0.0		0.0
Opening Stock					
Purchases					
Closing Stock					
Manufacturing expenses					
Wages					
COST OF SALES	0.0		0.0		0.0
GROSS PROFIT (as per books)	0.0		0.0		0.0
GROSS PROFIT (Excl. Non Business Income)	0.0		0.0		0.0
Administrative Expenses + any other exps					
Selling & Distribution Expenses					
Depreciation					
Interest to FI/Banks					
Interest to Pvt/Outside Parties					
Non cash exps written off (Prelim Exps/ Def. Rev Exp.)					
Salary to Partner/Director					
Interest Expenses paid to partners/director					
PROFIT BEFORE TAX (as per books)	0.0		0.0		0.0
PROFIT BEFORE TAX (Excl Non Business Inc)	0.0		0.0		0.0
Tax					
PAT (as per books)	0.0		0.0		0.0
PAT (Excl. Non Business Income)	0.0		0.0		0.0
CASH PROFITS (Excl Non Business Income)	0.0		0.0		0.0
Actual Cash Profit (Excl Non Business income)	0.0		0.0		0.0
PBDIT (Excl Non Biz Income, Incl. Rem/Sal Dir/Partners)	0.0		0.0		0.0
BALANCE SHEET		% Growth		% Growth	
LIABILITY	Rs. Lacs	#N/A	Rs. Lacs	#N/A	Rs. Lacs
Share Capital					
Reserves & Surplus(excluding revaluation reserve)					
Profit brought forward					
Total Net worth	0.0		0.0		0.0
Revaluation Reserve					
Adjusted Net worth	0.0		0.0		0.0
Long Term Loans from Banks/FI -AL					
Working Capital Limits from Banks/FIs					
Unsecured loans (Bank & Financial Institutions)					
TOTAL Outside borrowings	0.0		0.0		0.0
Unsecured loans from partners/shareholders (ICDs incl.)					
Current Liabilities & Provisions	0.0		0.0		0.0
Deferred tax Liability					
Sundry Creditors					
Other Liabilities					
Total Liabilities to outsiders	0.0		0.0		0.0
LIABILITY - TOTAL	0.0		0.0		0.0
ASSETS					
Plant & machinery					
Land & Building					
Other Fixed Assets					
Accumulated Depreciation					
Net Fixed Assets (Gross Fixed Assets - Accum. Dep)	0.0		0.0		0.0
Investments	0.0		0.0		0.0
Liquid/Marketable Investments (Biz Related)					
Group Co. Investments (Biz Related)					
Group Co. Investments (Not Biz Related)					
Unquoted/Dead Investments (Non Biz Related)					
Current Assets	0.0		0.0		0.0
Deferred Tax Asset					
Inventories					
Receivables / Debtors	0.0		0.0		0.0
Debtors > 6 months					
Debtors < 6 months					
Cash and Bank					
Loans & Advances	0.0		0.0		0.0
Loans & Adv. to directors/partners etc (ICDs)/Diversions					
Loans and Advances given to others (Biz Related)					
Misc Exp. (DRE+PreOp+Prelim+Acc P&L)					
ASSET - TOTAL	0.0		0.0		0.0

Growth Ratios :- Growth in Sales			
Growth in Net Profits (PAT)			
Profitability Ratios :- Gross Profit Margin Ratio			
Net Profit Margin Ratio			
Cash Profit Ratio			
Leverage Ratios :- Debt Equity Ratio			
Interest Coverage Ratio			
DSCR			
DSCR after the proposed Loan	0.00	0.00	0.000
TOL / TNW			
Current Ratio			
Working Capital Cycle :- Debtor Days			
Stock Days			
Creditor Days			
Net Working Capital Cycle			
CASH FLOW FROM OPERATING ACTIVITIES			
Net Profit Before Tax	0.00	0.00	0.00
Adjustments for:			
Depreciation	0.00	0.00	0.00
Non cash exps written off (Prelim Exps/ Def. Rev Exp.)	0.00	0.00	0.00
Interest & Finance Charges	0.00	0.00	0.00
Non Business Income (Dividend, Interest on FD,etc.)	0.00	0.00	0.00
Operating Profit before Working Capital Changes	0.00	0.00	0.00
Adjustments for:			
Decrease/(Increase) in Receivables	0.00	0.00	0.00
Decrease/(Increase) in Inventories	0.00	0.00	0.00
Decrease/(Increase) in Other Asset Deferred tax	0.00	0.00	0.00
Decrease/(Increase) in Misc. Exps.	0.00	0.00	0.00
Increase/(Decrease) in Payables	0.00	0.00	0.00
Increase/(Decrease) in Deferred tax liability	0.00	0.00	0.00
Cash generated from operations	0.00	0.00	0.00
Income Tax paid	0.00	0.00	0.00
Net Cash flow from Operating activities	0.00	0.00	0.00
CASH FLOW FROM INVESTING ACTIVITIES			
Sale / (Purchase) of Fixed Assets	0.00	0.00	0.00
Investments not related to business	0.00	0.00	0.00
Investments related to Business	0.00	0.00	0.00
Increase in Advances & others	0.00	0.00	0.00
Non Business Income (Dividend, Interest on FD,etc.)	0.00	0.00	0.00
Net Cash used in Investing activities	0.00	0.00	0.00
CASH FLOW FROM FINANCING ACTIVITIES			
Increase (Decrease) in Long term Borrowings	0.00	0.00	0.00
Increase (Decrease) in Networth	0.00	0.00	0.00
Increase (Decrease) in Funds from partners / directors	-	-	-
Interest paid	0.00	0.00	0.00
Net Cash used in financing activities	0.00	0.00	0.00
Net increase in cash & Cash Equivalents	0.00	0.00	0.00
Cash and Cash equivalents as at 01.04.....	0.00	0.00	0.00
Cash and Cash equivalents as at 31.03......	0.00	0.00	0.00
Balance should become Zero	0.00	0.00	0.00
Cash & Cash Equivalents			
Cash in Hand			
Cash at Bank			
Cash & Cash equivalents as stated			

Problems with financial statements and auditors

It is important to note that there are several difficulties in using the information in a company's financial statements.

- There is no complete and comprehensive set of accounting standards.

  For example, in the same industry, a transaction can be presented in several ways, all in accordance with AS. The analyst should be aware of the way a company is presenting its accounts.

- Financial statements represent the work of two parties — the directors/

management and the auditors – with differing interests. There will be differences of opinion that must be reconciled to the satisfaction of both parties.

- Published financial statements are prepared for a wide audience. In addition to the shareholders, the annual report is targeted towards institutional investors. analysts, employees, and the public.

- Accounting involves approximations. For example, it is difficult to value assets such as partially finished 'work-in-progress' or provisions for bad or doubtful debts.

- There are different methods of valuing assets. Current assets such as receivables. less provisions for doubtful debts, are often estimates. Likewise, stock/inventories can be valued in a number of different ways such as LIFO (Last In, First Out), FIFO (First In, First Out), WACM (weighted average cost method), etc.

- In accounting there are honest differences of opinion. There are also ambiguities enabling companies to manipulate accounts and misrepresent the true and fair state of their company and often the auditors are colluding with the company in signing off on financial statements known to be misleading if not outright fraudulent. The analyst should be aware that these exist and that accounting in recent years has become unreliable. This is not only a breakdown in accounting practice but indeed goes to the very heart of the ethos of accounting.

- Accounting terminology can vary. For example, income statement, P/L statement. statement of income and retained earnings, and operating statement are all different ways of referring to the same statement: stock can be called inventory. and debtors either receivables or accounts receivable. You should be familiar with the general characteristics of the accounting language.

- Accounting has evolved by convention and tradition over time, and that there are many anomalies and differences of opinion in the practice. Accounting attempts to quantify the approximate and at times unquantifiable.

One cannot blame individual corporations since they are merely falling in line with the prevailing business environment (which is the result of currently prevailing corporate fads masquerading as economic policy) in order not to be left behind its competitors. The blame must be shared by the governments and regulatory bodies which, under pressure from corporate lobbyists, approved more and more lenient accounting techniques that enabled firms to estimate future profits liberally, especially when the profits came from trading in derivatives.

Outside information

Due to limitation of accounting & problem in financial statements we cant 100% rely on it. So many other sources of information are available to supplement a company's financial statements. For bigger companies like listed company much of this information is free and easily obtainable in the public domain and over the Internet.

This information can be of a general macroeconomic nature such as industry studies from the ratings agencies such as fitch, crisil, care, care, onicra, samera etc.
It is a good idea therefore to bear in mind who is preparing this free information and why. In reality, 'free' does not exist, at least in a capitalist economy, and if this information is being provided 'free of charge', that is usually because it is satisfying someone's agenda

Such data should provide enough information to develop a complete picture of the company, its operations, and management. The normal scope of a credit analysis requires that a substantial amount of verified and consistent data be available on which to base a decision. Moreover, the use of such information should be cited so that the reader can make his own mind up about the validity or not of the information.

Information available direct from the borrower

The purpose of information is to enable effective credit decisions to be made, so that costly lending errors can be avoided. It is important there- fore that information be reliable. Consider the essential information which is obtained directly from members of senior management, such as the CEO or finance director. How reliable is this information?
It is normal to ask oneself how accurate such financial statements are likely to be both during a best case scenario (inflating corporate performance to please share and rating analysts) as well as a worst case scenario (hiding fraud). Moreover, one can pose the question of whether the company's auditors are colluding in the fraud in an effort to retain profitable business and indeed sell more profitable 'consulting' business (for example, many of the fraudulent mechanisms present in stayam were designed by PWC, its auditors.

This type of information can be crucial, not only in assessing the credit- worthiness of the customer, but indeed their mentality, as well as evaluating and minimizing the risks involved in documentation relating to the loan, and in claiming assets in the event of default.

Meeting with borrower

At the time of meeting with the borrower analyst should match the set up with the financial statements. Whether no of machineries is matching with the fixed assets showing in Balance sheet, amount of wages is matching with no of workers, raw material is matching with as per books, and most important is turnover matching with books. He should also focus on behavior of borrower like professionalism, way of replying of queries etc. After meeting analyst makes him comfortable whether he has any question as to the integrity, honesty or good intention of borrower.

Bank and trade enquiries

A credit analyst should check internal bank records in the case of an existing or previous customer to see if the account has functioned smoothly, as well as enquiries made to the company's other banks. Direct enquiries can also be made with both suppliers and customers whose names can be provided by the borrower (for example by asking for a list of the company's 10 largest debtors and creditors – or accounts receivable and payable).

For example, a company could have changed its corporate structure, dismissed certain members of management, sold or acquired a subsidiary, entered into an alliance or cooperative agreement with a competitor to market or distribute a product, or availed itself of the services of a rival bank in closing a transaction.

Credit reporting and rating agencies

Agencies such as Dun & Bradstreet and Standard and Poor provide commercial credit ratings as well as reports on a one-off basis if required. There may also be domestic credit reporting services operating in the country in question. Trade payment information can be obtained from agencies on a subscription basis, but you should be familiar with the characteristics of such reports and interpret them accordingly.

Industry information

Publications containing abbreviated financial data and ratios of companies in a business or industry can be useful in evaluating peer group averages of sales growth, stock turnover, or profitability:

- Bloomberg
- The Economist
- Business Today
- Periodicals

You should regularly refer to the web sites of business newspapers such as the The Economic times, Financial Times, money control, The Economist, or business publications of the country within which the company in question is based.

Since the web is in constant evolution, any interesting articles should be indexed and saved locally in a specialized directory regrouping all relevant articles featuring on the company for future reference since the web page may go offline in future. It s important to note details such as the author, publication, and publication date should the source need to be cited in future. All relevant data can be burned onto a CD for placing in the credit file.

Credit Risks

Introduction to Credit risks

Credit risk arises whenever a lender exposed to loss from a borrower. Counterparty or an obligor who fails to honor their debt obligation as they agreed & contracted. For lenders who extend credit in the form of loans, trading activities or the capital markets credit risk is inherent in all their business activities and is an element in virtually every product & services that is provided.

The risks in lending to a borrower can be summarized as follows:

According to Ernst & Young's research, non-financial performance indica- tors drive at least 35% of investor decisions, as depicted in the graph below:

Let's discuss all risks in details

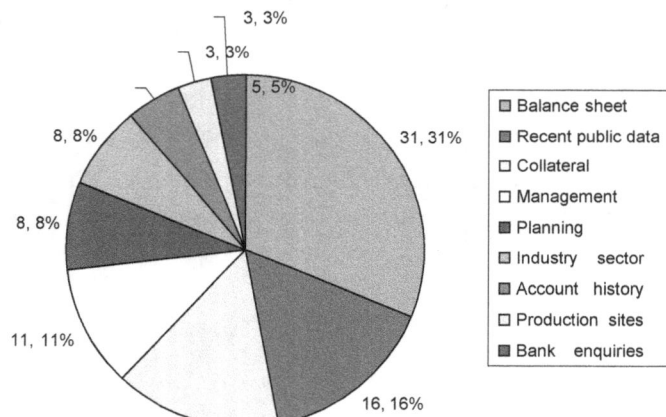

Factors influencing the lending decision

Borrower risk

actually lending money or giving a period of time for payment of an obligation, to relying upon the other entity to satisfy or perform another form of financial obligation, for example, the successful completion of a project or the provision of adequate collateral. Borrower risk represent risks which must be assessed and understood for what they are prior to committing funds

I. Business risk – the generic business and environment risks the bor- rower is subject to in its day-to-day operating environment. Accurately assessing a borrower's creditworthiness in the light of the economic environment is therefore crucial if the bank is to be a successful lender.

II. Financial risk traditionally focuses on elements surrounding the borrower and his financial situation. This includes analyzing elements such as the nature of the obligor (limited vs. unlimited liability), financial performance indices (which we will consider later) and management effectiveness in managing successive business cycles as evidenced by financial stability.

Transaction risk

Once the borrower (financial and environment) risk analysis is completed, the facility structure needs to be set in place appropriately (in light of the borrower's condition). This is known as the transaction risk. The facility needs to be structured so that it works smoothly, especially in a complex multi-currency cross-border syndicated loan (facility risk).

I. Facility risk represents the risks inherent in the facility itself, from ongoing management of a complicated transaction such as multi- trench multi-currency syndicated loan with many participants, prorate interest calculations, and coordination's of draw downs and repayments, as well as hedging of interest and currency rate variations.

II. Documentation risk – defining and controlling the structure of the loan facility is achieved via drafting appropriate loan documentation which is enforceable. The risks arising from improperly drafted loan documentation is known as documentation risk. While legal documentation is a subject of study in itself, we will touch on some of the more basic matters of legal and documentation risks as they relate to the financial analyst (in drafting loan covenants and assessing security for example) as well as the role of auditors.

The method of analysis required varies from borrower to borrower. It also varies in function of the type of lending being considered

For example, the banking risks in financing the building of a hotel or rail project, of providing lending secured by assets, or a large overdraft for a retail customer, would use the same risk model but the breakdown of those risks would vary considerably.

For example:

- For financing a project, you would mainly look at future cash flows generated by the project (cash-flow risk and documentation risk);
- For asset secured lending, you would look at the assets and ability to claim those assets (quality of assets and documentation risk);

For an overdraft facility, you would look at the way the account has been run over the past few years (facility risk).

In making the decision to take a risk and extend credit, it is important to understand and minimize that risk as far as possible. This requires a sys- tem to categorize and isolate individual elements of risk in order to fully assess them.

4 Business risk

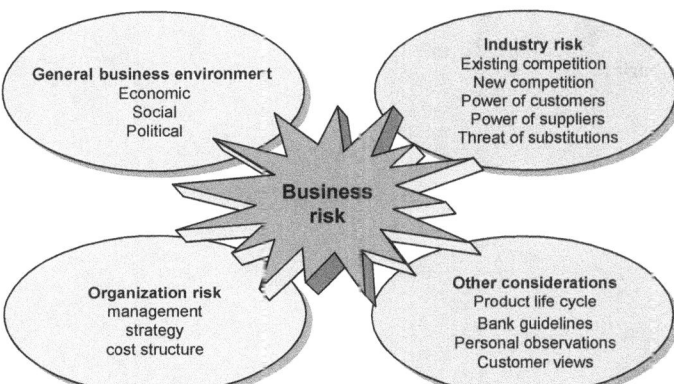

Framework for business risk analysis

General business environment
Economic
Social
Political

Industry risk
Existing competition
New competition
Power of customers
Power of suppliers
Threat of substitutions

Business risk

Organization risk
management
strategy
cost structure

Other considerations
Product life cycle
Bank guidelines
Personal observations
Customer views

Business risk can be understood by analyzing following non financial macro & micro economic risk areas:

Macro Economic risk areas:

1) Understanding of Environment
    i) Political/Regulatory/Legal
    ii) Economic
    iii) Social
    iv) Technological

2) Understanding of nature of obligor
3) Understanding of Industry
4) Understanding of Product
5) Understanding of Market
6) Understanding of Manufacturing/Production process

Micro Economic risk Areas

1) Management
2) Infrastructure/Set-up
    a) L&B
    b) P&M
    c) Employee/Workers
3) Real estate position of Promoters
4) Future plan & corporate strategy

Questioning techniques

Who, What, Where, When, Why, and How

In order to fully understand and interpret the information obtained it is useful to have a structured method of questioning.

A successful technique is to apply to the whole and to every component to be analyzed, a series of standard questions. The answers to the questions will often then identify another aspect or component which should be further investigated. By applying the questions again, and if necessary again, a full and detailed understanding can be obtained.

Experience will enable the analyst to develop his or her own systems of enquiry. The tried and tested journalist questions are a good starting point:

- Who?
- What?
- Where?
- When?
- Why?
- How?

Example:

Consider reviewing the most recent historic balance sheet of a business, particularly accounts receivables or debtors.

The questions are applied:

- Who owes the money to the business?

  – Answer – Obtain a list of debtors.

- What do they owe to the business?

  – Answer – Identify outstanding and any particular concentrations.

- Where are the clients which form accounts receivable based, are there any particular concentrations, domestic or international?

  – Answer – Identify any particular concentrations of debtors (e.g. 40% come from two clients; 75% are due from foreign clients …).

- When was the receivable created? How long has each been outstanding? Have they been paid when due?

  – Answer – an analysis showing time by client and amount is provided.

- Why do they owe the money to the business?

  – Answer – Identify which amounts relate to products sold on credit, and which relate to services provided.

- How are the accounts receivable to be settled? What are the terms of trade?

  – Answer – The domestic receivables are all on export account like PCL, PSL etc. The exports receivables are 50% export account (payment of invoice in the future) and 50% or documents against payment, or collection basis.

The responses have provided a significant amount of understanding of the activity of the potential obligor.

The example shows how, by repeatedly applying a routine series of simple questions, a substantial insight and understanding can be obtained. The analyst will, with experience, establish a routine to obtain sufficient information and understanding.

Whilst it is important to pursue all significant aspects of the credit, it should be noted that this technique can result in an information over- load. It is the analyst's responsibility to ensure that the proposal is not overanalyzed to the extent that a decision or opinion is either never reached or that the decision deadline is missed.

Let's discuss about every factors in details by using the questioning techniques

Macro-economic risk areas

1. Understanding of Environment

Environmental risks can be summarized by the acronym PEST which stands for *Political, economic, Social, Technological*. We shall consider some questions to ask when analyzing these environ mental risk categories.

i) Political/regulatory/legal

- Does the government restrict entry to the market? (E.g. by awarding concessions)
- Do governments impose import quotas/tariffs on the products?
- Are there government grants or subsidies available? In a global market how do these compare to those available to the competition?
- Does the government impose duty or taxes on the products?
- Are there regulatory requirements? (E.g. for safety, consumer protection, and free competition reasons)
- Are companies in the industry exposed to lawsuits which could have a material adverse effect on any individual company? e.g. product liability claims (e.g. tyre manufacturer, pharmaceutical companies), passenger liability claims (e.g. airlines), pollution claims (e.g. oil and chemical companies) and employee death/accident claims (e.g. oil exploration and production companies).

These risks can be mitigated through insurance. However, claims, particularly in the US, have

in some instances limited the maximum cover the insurance market is prepared to provide.

ii) Economic

- How is your company and the industry in which it operates affected by high interest rates?
- How does this impact on customer demand as well as the necessity to make higher interest payments.
- How is the industry/company affected by fluctuating foreign exchange rates? (Such fluctuations are important with a company that for example has its costs in GBP but sales in EUR and USD.)

1. New competitors – any company can lose market share to competitors and needs to be aware of developments which may affect it.

- How cyclical is the industry?
- How does the industry relate to the general economic cycle? Does it lead or lag the economic cycle, or is it countercyclical? (To check this, try to evaluate the company's performance over the last economic cycle or past 5–10 years)
- How is the industry affected by high inflation rates?
- How price-elastic are the industry's products and its raw materials?

iii) Social

- Is the industry inherently stable?
- Is the industry affected (either positively or negatively) by changes in social tastes or fashions?

a) Product substitution is another risk — customers may become disen- chanted with one product and favour an alternative (e.g. buses instead of trains).

b) Market demand for its products — a shift in consumer perceptions or needs can impact the demand for the company's products.

■ Are there 'green' issues? What is the industry's record on pollution?

iv) Technological

Technological issues affect the industry/company in two main ways:

- Firstly, is the product obsolete and likely to be superseded by a better new product? ('Better' might be in terms of price or quality.)
- Has there been a fundamental change in the cost structure of manufacturing the product?

2) Nature of the obligor

It is important to understand the nature of the borrower if the technical analysis is to be valid. The understanding of the nature of the obligor can be split into two components:

- Its formal or legal nature (on the basis of Limited liability, Unlimited liability, Trusts, Society etc) and
- Its general standing (in the industry, locality, country or internationally).

The formal or legal structure of the obligor, whether an entity incorporated with limited liability (e.g. a Public Limited Company (PLC), or limited company) or an entity without limited liability (e.g. a partnership or sole trader) will each have differing legal implications, responsibilities and risks.

Without an understanding of the legal nature of the obligor there exists a possibility that any debt or obligation could never be enforced legally against the obligor.

The legal nature of the entity defines specific aspects of the risk profile:

- ' Who' and 'What ' the obligor entity is;
- ' Where', 'When', 'Why' – how it may operate;
- 'How' and 'Why' could the obligation be avoided and
- 'What ' implications are there in situations where the debt needs to be recovered.

We can understand the various risks on the basis of nature of obligor:

No	Particular	Limited Co (Pvt /Public)	Sole Proprietorship/ Partnership
1.	Liabilities	Limited to shares only	Unlimited
2.	Governing Body	Companies Act 1956	Prop-NA, Partnership Act 1932(optional)
3.	Public documents(like FS, Shareholder etc)	Available by paying nominal fees	Not available
4.	Audit	Mandatory	Only if turnover >60 lakh/20 lac
5.	Compliances	Very high	Nominal
7.	Creation of charge	Available	Not available
6.	Winding Up	Complicated	Easy

So by above difference we can understand easily that Sole proprietorship & Partnerships firms are more risky compare to Ltd companies.

Note: Non-profit organization like hospital, school, trust, society etc is incorporated & governs by provisions of under its respective act i.e. Indian trust act, society registration Act etc.

It is important, therefore, particularly when dealing with entities incorp orated in a jurisdiction where the analyst is not fully conversant with the local law, that a full understanding is obtained – if necessary, via expert local legal advice so that any loan contract be fully effective.

For minimizing the risks

It is important to obtain independent data from the registration authority (i.e. MCA) which will show the current formal status of the entity in terms of its share capital structure, its controlling documents, often the names of the officers or directors, and sometimes their respective shareholdings and any other directorships they may hold will be disclosed. Any information obtained independently from this type of 'search' of the registration information, will provide a further insight into the obligor (and possibly its directors and owners).

Negative list of industries

Other factors may have an effect upon the decision to grant credit. Investors subject to 'green' guidelines may be favorable to lending to entities such as society, trust or not give credit to another entity which does not operate in an environmentally friendly way like beauty parlor, lawyer, media personalities etc. *(Details as per Annexure 1)*

The following matrix helps to bear in mind the significance of the answers to the various questions above in assessing management acumen and the likely results of future performance.

Management strategy – operations relationship

	Clear	Unclear
Effective	**I** Clear strategy and effective operations have equalled success in the past and will in the future	**II** Unclear strategy but effective operations have equalled success in the past but success is doubtful in the future
Ineffective	**III** Clear strategy but ineffective operations have sometimes worked in the past in the short run but increased competition makes success doubtful in the future	**IV** Unclear strategy and ineffective operations have equalled failure in the past and will in the future

3. Understanding the industry

The industry sector in which the borrower operates will have significant impact upon the way the business is managed. It will also produce different financing and asset structures in the balance sheet of the business. The exact nature of the industry and the differentiation within each industry sector will develop the basis for understanding the other components in this section as they are all interlinked. The terms of trade which exist between the buyer and the seller in the industry and the methods by which the contracts of sale are controlled both legally and practically will all have an effect upon the borrower's activity in the industry and a financial implication in its business.

Understanding the industry – some questions

- What is the nature of the industry? (E.g. heavy or light industrial, services or financial).
- Is it based upon high or low technology? Is it at the forefront of tech- nological development? (E.g. new microchip production) or is it based upon relatively simple techniques used for many years (e.g. metal pipe production).
- What form does the industry take, does it relate to a manufactured product or to a service?
- Is it a capital intensive industry requiring substantial investment in plant and equipment? (e.g. steel production) or relatively low capital investment (e.g. engineering consultancy).
- Is the industry vulnerable to changes in fashion or is it classical?
- In times of economic change will it suffer or contract? What is the growth potential?
- What stability exists in the industry?
- Where is the industry located?

- What legal limitations exist which influence the industry? (e.g. Health and safety regulations, environmental legislations

4. Understanding the markets

The nature of the market in which the customer operates or in which its products are sold is important to understand. It has a major influence on the level and style of activity and the financial results. In investigating the market the analyst will be able to establish a point of view of both macro- and micro-economic elements that may affect the future of the debtor or obligor. In addition significant understanding of the potential effectiveness of plans and strategies can be achieved when comparing the obligors' view of the market compared to independently sourced information.

Understanding the market – some questions

- Where are the markets for the products or services?
- Is the market large or small?
- Is the market local, national or international?
- What affects the supply and demand in the market?
- How large is the market and what is the obligor's current and antici- pated market share?
- What section of the total market does it operate within?
- Who are the competitors?
- How substantial is the competition? In financial and resource strength, existing market share?
- Does the obligor have a reliance on one market, or one sector?
- Does the obligor have dominance in the market?
- Is the market really quantifiable? How? When and Who by?
- Where can reliable independent verification be obtained?
- What will be the effect of a change in technology?
- Is there cyclicality in the market? A volatility in demand?
- What freedom is there in the sales pricing structure?
- What is the position of the obligor? (e. g. manufacturer, distributor, and retailer).
- What timescales exist in the market? (e. g. compares ship construction to dairy processing milk).

5. Understanding the products

The nature of the product may be physical or intangible. Physical products may be the result of a repetitive process (whether simple or complex) or the result of a specific 'tailor made' process. It is important to understand the different nature of the processes and the potential risks involved in the production. The production risk will vary dependent upon its specialty and size.

Understanding the products – some questions

- What are the products?
- Are they the result of a physical process (e.g. manufacturing) or a technical, academic process (e.g. training or consulting).

- Where and how are they produced or sourced?
- Are they proven or new products?
- Are they staple products (e.g. bread, soap, etc.) or are they luxury, specialist or speculative in their nature?
- Are they standard and therefore repetitive in production or are they special production (one-offs).
- What is the nature of supplies of raw materials?
- Is the product perishable?
- How long does the product take to make?
- Is it labour intensive or automated?

6. Understanding manufacturing/performance risk

Manufacturing and performance risk are another risk category. All companies undertaking business operations are subjected to this risk. For example, manufacturing risk can relate to the ability of the company to successfully manage production cycles without experiencing negative tendencies. A car manufacturer for example will have several aspects relating to manufacturing risk: work stoppages, machinery breakdown, faulty cars needing recall, etc. Similarly, a manufacturer of LCD screens may experience a higher than acceptable rate of manufacturing defects, thereby adversely impacting profitability.

Performance risk is similar but focuses more on service oriented com- panies, for example can the company successfully manage the hotel or air- line in question? If the ongoing performance management of the business is unacceptable, then the business will be correspondingly impacted.

It is for the analyst to carefully consider the nature of the business and identify the key manufacturing risks involved in order to ascertain the manufacturing and performance risks involved.

Understanding manufacturing/performance risk – some questions

- What is manufacturing risk?
- What is the difference between manufacturing risk and performance risk?
- Is financial statement analysis appropriate in analyzing manufacturing risk?
- Is the company's management team up to the task of managing manufacturing risk?
- Is analyzing management appropriate in analyzing performance risk?
- Is an aircraft manufacture more concerned by manufacturing risk or performance risk?
- Is a supermarket more concerned by manufacturing risk or performance risk?

Micro-economicrisk areas

1. Understanding of management

If a business is not effectively managed and the senior managers do not have the skills to manage all components of the business, it will fail.

One of the skills of these senior managers will be reflected in their ability to structure the organization with appropriate junior level managers or supervisors. Quality of management may have a significant effect upon the future success of the business it is the overall view that will lead the analyst to satisfactory conclusion. Again, application of the questioning techniques will lead to a good understanding of each of the components.

Some questions you may want to ask about the company's management are as follows:

Structure, responsibilities, and succession

– What is the management structure?

– Who has what responsibilities?

– Is there a skills spread appropriate to managing the business? (finance, marketing, production, delivery, and human resources),

– Are there the necessary general management skills to bring individual skills together?

– Are there sufficient industry specific skills in the group?

– What is the structure and interrelationship between executive and non-executive management.

  – Is it effective?

  – How have the management team performed overall?

  – Have there been substantial or frequent changes in management?

2. Infrastructure (Set up)

Analyst should analyze the set up of the business whether it is aligned with the financial statements. For example, plant & machinery, land & building, turnover, workers etc. As there may be scenario that borrower not showing actual turnover in the books for paying for lesser taxes to government. So by analyzing the infrastructure (i.e. set up) he can understand better his actual position.

i) Land and buildings

The nature of the business premises used and the plans for the future will affect the ongoing future health of the business. The practical adequacy and suitability of the buildings in the short and medium term is clearly paramount.

Any aspects of the business activity which may create legal or community obligations and responsibilities should be understood.

For example, a business dealing in toxic chemical products for example must have suitable premises and controls in place.

Some questions to ask regarding land and buildings are as follows:

- Is the usage of the building freehold, leasehold or rental?
- If leasehold or rental, how long will the premises be available?
- What contingency plans do management have if a move is necessary?
- What value is there in the buildings?
- What is the market value compared with the study material or accounting value?
- Is there adequate insurance coverage?
- What financial obligations do the premises have.
- Is there a specific debt which financed the purchase?
- What are the financial obligations under the lease or rental agreement?

ii) Plant and machinery

The fundamental quality, age and general condition of the equipment used in the business will affect the overall financial performance.

The effect of the introduction of new technology in the industry, making the borrower's product no longer cost effective for its customer will significantly impact future prosperity.

The capacity of the existing equipment compared to the expectations and demand of the productive activity need to be questioned and understood.

A business using older equipment, even if reliable, will have more main tenance and therefore non-productive time, compared to a business using newer equipment.

Some questions to ask are as follows:

- ❖ *The value of the equipment (market and study material or accounting value)*
- ❖ *Any debt or obligations relating to the equipment must be investigated (especially if equipment is not owned or is subject to leasing or hire purchase agreements).*
- ❖ *The necessity for some equipment is worth questioning. For example in small businesses with modest performance and profit (or losses) is it really necessary for all the directors and managers to have cars?*

iii) Real estate position of Promoters

In SME sector where majority of companies are owned by family members only. And out of which 54% is in proprietorship & partnership firms. There may be a scenario where borrower shows the lower profit for paying of lower taxes. But in actual it may be high. It can analyze by its real estate Value generated by him.

Some questions to ask regarding land and buildings are as follows:

a. Is property self generated or inherited
b. Is there any property, which is recently purchased or being purchased.
c. Ownership of the property(i.e. self , wife or parents)
d. Details of property added after joining the business
e. Address, location of all property
f. Area & total Value of property

iv) Corporate strategy and future plans

To define corporate plans, management has to determine the starting point and the ultimate goal. This typically begins by defining a strategy to take the business from one specific point to another in the future and achieve certain goals such as making the business grow. This entails identifying both macro- and micro-economic factors, and the opportunities/risks for the business in a specific market, and then addresses each component with a solution to affect successful entry into the market. This will set the strategy for the business and an outline for the next stage which is practical planning

5 Financial risks

Financial statement analysis

This chapter on financia risks statement analysis begins with an introduction to financial statement analysis and discussion on the purpose and use of company annual accounts.

It then takes a detailed look at the background to the annual report and accounts including the background to the Companies Acts, auditor's report, director's report and Statement of accounting Policies, notes to accounts.

The balance sheet is then treated thematically, covering the principal accounts:

- Debtors,
- Creditors,
- Stock And Work In Progress,
- Borrowings,
- Fixed Assets,
- Share Capital
- Reserves

The chapter then examines the workings of the profit and loss (P/L) account and cash flow statements and ends with a simple ratio analysis and discussion of the limitations of published accounts.

It also examines the content and relevance of tax auditor report, ITR, Memorandum of Association (MOA), Article of association (AOA), Performa invo ces, Vat return, analysis of bank statement, KYC etc.

Introduction to financial statement analysis

What is the goal of a corporate credit analysis? One answer is that it is to assess an obligor from a financial perspective to confirm that he will be able to meet his obligations when they are due, to identify the potential risks, and to perfect the security and collateral and loan documentation in crder opt mally to manage these inherent risks.

This chapter aims to give you an overview of the financial statements that companies produce, why they produce them and what their   constituent parts are by using concrete examples and i lustrations.

Company accounts follow certain standards in their content and presentation. Whilst these statements may appear to be confusing to the newcomer, or ce dissected and recast into a standardized spreadsheet presentation, the financial statements can provide answers to a wide range of questions and help a prospective lender reach certain decisions about the company and the nature of our relationship with it.

The annual report and accounts

About published accounts

The emergence of the large scale limited liability company has been the single most important factor stimulating the need for financial reports.

The larger and more complex the company the more remote the   management can become from day-to-day operations, and the more reliant they become on accounting information.

In addition, companies that borrow money will need to demonstrate their financial solidity to its bankers, and financial statements are used by bankers and others as part of the basis for lending decisions.

Many different parties have a legitimate interest in a company's performance, for example:

- Equity investors – existing and potential shareholders.
- Loan creditors – existing and potential holders of debentures and loan stock, and providers of short-term unsecured loans and finance.
- The company's bankers.
- The company's employees.
- The analysts/advisers – this will include financial analysts and journalists, economists, researchers, stockbrokers, etc.
- Customers, trade creditors, and suppliers.
- Tax authorities, supervisory bodies, and local authorities.
- The general public – including taxpayers, consumers, political parties, consumer and environmental groups.

Each of the groups has a common interest in financial statements of a company but will use the information as the basis for different types of decisions.

There are differences in the amount of financial information made available to each of these groups, caused by different legal requirements and the company 's management decisions as to what they wish to make available and to each group.

Introduction

All companies produce an annual report and accounts.

The style and content of the annual report and accounts vary considerably from company to company. Often, in case of listed companies the annual report is an exercise in graphical arts design and a flattering self-promoting presentation of the company's activities – making it effectively a marketing exercise.

However, there is a minimum amount of information that the law requires a company to print in the report and accounts.

The four basic components required are as follows:

- The directors' report,
- A report by the company's auditors,
- A balance sheet and a p/l account,
- A statement of accounting policies and notes to the accounts.

Companies listed on the Stock Exchange have to produce a half- yearly, interim, report. Their annual report and accounts have to contain more information than for unlisted companies.

The Companies Acts

The Companies Acts 1956 imposes certain requirements on companies and their directors:

- Directors have a legal responsibility to prepare and publish accounts which give a 'true and fair' view of their company s financial affairs.
- Company accounts must be put before its members at the annual general meeting (AGM), and must be circulated beforehand to all share- holders, debenture holders, and any other persons entitled to attend the AGM.
- Directors must file a copy of the company's accounts with the Registrar of Companies, where they will be available for public inspection (small and medium size private companies may present abridged versions because they do not require the same level scrutiny as larger, public companies).
- Accounts must be delivered to the Registrar within a time limit fixed by reference to its accounting year end. The limit for a public company is 7 months from its accounting year end. The Stock Exchange requires listed companies to issue an annual report within 6 months of the date of their financial year end.

Filing information with the Registrar of Companies

Companies are also required to file the following information with the
Registrar of Companies:

- copies of their Memorandum and Articles of Association, and details of subsequent changes;
- address of their registered office, and the place at which the company's registers are kept;
- details of the company's share capital and debentures;
- details of each mortgage and charge on the assets of the company(ROC)
- a list of the directors and secretary and any changes.

Companies' files are now maintained at the company's registration office and on line, it can also be viewed on payment of a small fee *(www.mcagov.in)*

The Companies Act requires companies to file annual returns, which contain a summary of points 2–5 along with a list of past and present members. Every 3 years a list is prepared of shareholders and it is therefore possible to find out, who has been a registered shareholder of the company.

Presentation of financial statements

There are various methods available for valuing and accounting for business assets and liabilities. It is therefore important that the   company states which policies have been used in preparing the accounts in order to enable the reader correctly to interpret the company's financial statements.

For example, the way in which a company's assets are valued has direct implications for the level of reported profits.

The companies act 1956 adopted all of the Accounting Standard recommended by ICAI and in addition have been issuing further accounting standards, which are known as International Financial Reporting Standards (IFRS).

The Accounting Standard and IFRS are guidelines for the production of company financial statements by ICAI and some of their recommendations have been incorporated into the Companies Acts and have the force of law.

Accounting premises
Company accounts are based on the following four premises:

- *The going concern concept*: This assumes that the company will continue in business for the foreseeable future. The main effect of this   assumption is that the liquidation value of fixed assets (which may be significantly different from the study material value) may be ignored.
- *The accruals (or matching) concept*: This requires that the revenues be matched with related expenses when measuring profit and that revenues and expenses be included in the P/L account as they are earned and incurred rather than when they are received and paid.
- *The consistency concept*: This requires the company to use the same accounting policies for valuing similar assets both within the accounting period and during consecutive accounting periods.
- *The concept of prudence*: This states that companies should not   anticipate profits, but requires them to provide for all foreseeable losses.

Accounting policies

This is the term used to describe the accounting bases chosen by a particu- lar company for the purposes of valuing assets and liabilities.

The accounting policies on which a company's accounts are based are shown at the beginning of the notes to the accounts, and typically will include the basis of accounting for:

- sales,

- deferred taxation,
- depreciation of fixed assets,
- investment grants,
- research and development,
- stocks and work in progress,
- extraordinary items,
- translation of foreign currencies.

THE AUDITOR'S REPORT

Auditor's rights

Every company is required to appoint during the AGM, an auditor to hold office from the date of that meeting until the next AGM. This will usually be a firm of accountants.

The Companies Act 1956 made it an offence for a director or company secretary of a company to give false or misleading statements to their auditor.

The auditor has right of access at all times to the study materials and accounts of the company and can require any information and explanations from the officers of the company as he or she thinks fit and necessary for the performance of the auditor's duties.

The auditor also has the right to attend any general meetings and to speak on any part of the business which concerns him or her.

Auditor's duties

The auditor is required to report to the shareholders of the company whether in their opinion the balance sheet, P/L and other financial statements have been properly prepared in accordance with legislation and if they give a true and fair view of the profitability and state of affairs of the company.

If they feel that the accounts have not been properly prepared; that the records do not accord with fact and/or they have not been able to obtain all the information that they need in order to give an informed opinion they must state this in their report; this is known as qualifying the audit report.

Summary

The auditor's report covers information contained in the three main financial statements: the P/L account; the balance sheet; and the cash flow statement. In preparing their report the auditor is also required to consider whether the information contained in the directors' report is consistent with the accounts, and if it is not, they are required to say so.

It is important to note that the auditor's report does not certify the accuracy of the accounts, but expresses the opinion that the accounts show a true and fair view of the company.

Auditor's opinion

An auditor's report should contain a clear expression of opinion on a company's financial statements. The opinion will be:

- **An unqualified opinion.** Everything appears to be in order as laid down by the Institute of Chartered Accountants of India.

- **A qualified opinion.** This will be expressed by the auditor when there is either:
- a limitation on the scope of the auditors examination of the com- pany's accounts and affairs;
- if the auditor disagrees with the way a matter has been treated or disclosed in the financial statements.

- **An adverse opinion** expressed by the auditor if their disagreement with the company is so material or pervasive that they feel that the company 's accounts are seriously misleading and do not give a true and fair view of the company's situation.

Other opinions

- A disclaimer of opinion. This is expressed by the auditor when the pos- sible effect of a limitation on the scope of the audit is so material that the auditor has been unable to obtain sufficient material to support or express any opinion on the financial statements.
- Fundamental uncertainty. Where an inherent uncertainty exists which in the auditor's opinion is fundamental and is adequately accounted for and disclosed in the accounts, the auditor will include an explanatory paragraph in their report, making it clear that their opinion is not qualified by this.

The Directors Report

The content of the directors' report is laid down by the Companies Act. These may include, where relevant to the company's activities, sections on:

- Results and dividends.
- Review of the business.
- Market value of land and buildings, fixed assets.
- Research and development; future developments.
- Events since the end of last year.
- Directors' names and their interests in the share capital of the company.
- Political and charitable contributions.
- Transfers to and from reserves.

The contents of the directors' report can be classified into three categories:

- Information required by law – e.g. the review of the year.
- Information required by the Stock Exchange (for listed companies).
- Voluntary information – additional useful comments.

Statutory requirements

Under the Companies Acts, a directors' report must give the following information:

- A fair review of the development of the business during the year and an indication of likely future developments.
- The names of the directors and details of their interests in the shares of the company.
- Important events which have occurred since the end of the year (post balance sheet events).
- Significant changes in fixed assets
  2. Material changes and commitments, if, any affecting the financial position of the company which have incurred between the end of financial year and the date of report
- Political or charitable donations.
- Details of any repurchase of the company's shares by the company during the year.

1. Every employee having remuneration is more than 24 lakh per annum for the financial year or 2 lakh per month, if employed for a part of the year.

2. Changes in class of changes

3. Disqualification of directors

Stock Exchange requirements

There also exist additional reporting requirements in the annual report and accounts for the directors' report of listed companies, designed to protect shareholders' interests:

Notes to the financial statements

These can offer important information not appearing on the balance sheet, such as a breakdown of the various accounts, impending law suits arising from product liability (e.g. unsafe cars), environmental issues (e.g. radioactive leakage or oil spills), or patents. Normally, litigation or regulatory actions must be disclosed in the notes to the financial statements as a 'contingent liability'. However, in some cases, an estimated amount of the liability may not be disclosed because the company feels that calculating the potential liability could be viewed as a tacit admittance of liability. Again, it is for the analyst to examine the information in order to assess the potential impact of such developments.

And there are several methods in accounting policies like Dep method or disclosure requirement as per accounting standards like related party disclosure, arms length price etc of which financial statement are prepared required to show in notes to accounts.

The Balance Sheet
Introduction

The balance sheet is one of the basic components of the company's report and accounts. It is a statement of the assets (what the company owns) and liabilities (what the company owes) of a company at the close of business on a stated date, 'the balance sheet date'.

The balance sheet shows:

- How cash is invested in the business
- How the assets are balanced with the liabilities
- How the company is financed

When a company is formed its members subscribe for shares. For example, in our simple balance sheet(given below) there is a figure of Rs. 250,000 shown as ordinary share capital (we will discuss different types of shares later in this chapter); this represents the total sum which the members of the company have between them contributed to get the company started.

The cash raised by issuing these shares will be used in the business to buy fixed assets, such as an office or factory for the company's operations, to buy machinery and other fixed assets such as motor cars, and to buy stock ready to start trading.

Share capital itself may not suffice to pay all of the company's initial costs and to enable it to start trading. For example in the balance sheet there may be various liabilities such as 'overdraft', various negotiated credit terms with suppliers that do not require immediate payment and hence become creditors of the company.

SIMPLE BALANCE SHEET

Liabilities	Amount	Assets	Amount
Capital	100000	Fixed Assets	220000
Reserve & Surplus	20000		
Unsecured Loan	50000	Prepaid expenses	10000
Secured Loan	40000		
		Debtors	10000
Sundry Creditors	30000		
		Closing Stock	10000
Expenses payable	10000		
	250000		250000

On the assets side we have various categories of assets such as current assets, fixed assets, and intangible assets.

The balance sheet will always balance, that is the figure for total liabilities (Rs.250,000) must always be the same as for total assets – if it is not, something has been missed or wrongly accounted for.

BALANCE SHEET *(sample)*

BALANCE SHEET	FY 10-11	% Growth	FY 09-10	% Growth	FY 08-09
LIABILITY	Rs. Lacs	#N/A	Rs. Lacs	#N/A	Rs. Lacs
Share Capital	5.0	0.0%	5.0	0.0%	5.0
Reserves & Surplus(excluding revaluation reserve)	19.9	125.8%	8.8	9.1%	8.1
Profit brought forward					
Total Net worth	24.9	80.2%	13.8	5.6%	13.1
Revaluation Reserve					
Adjusted Net worth	**81.3**	22.9%	**66.1**	24.9%	**52.9**
Long Term Loans from Banks/FI -AL	31.9	-1.6%	32.4	192.5%	11.1
Working Capital Limits from Banks/FI's	23.1	-8.5%	25.2	45.9%	17.3
Unsecured loans (Bank & Financial Institutions)					
TOTAL Outside borrowings	**55.0**	-4.6%	**57.7**	103.1%	**28.4**
Unsecured loans from partners/shareholders (ICDs incl.)	57.9	7.6%	53.8	30.8%	41.1
Current Liabilities & Provisions	38.1	-16.5%	45.6	29.2%	35.3
Deferred tax Liability	0.1	-44.7%	0.2		
Sundry Creditors	24.8	-35.7%	38.6	32.8%	29.1
Other Liabilities	13.1	94.2%	6.8	8.8%	6.2
Total Liabilities to outsiders	93.0	-9.9%	103.2	62.1%	63.7
LIABILITY - TOTAL	**175.8**	2.9%	**170.8**	44.9%	**117.9**
ASSETS					
Plant & machinery	45.0		30.8		2.81
Land & Building	47.6		82.4		73
Other Fixed Assets	8.7	136.7%	3.7	-18.5%	4.5
Accumulated Depreciation	7.0	119.5%	3.2	118.2%	1.5
Net Fixed Assets (Gross Fixed Assets - Accum. Dep)	**94.3**	-17.0%	**113.6**	44.0%	**78.9**
Investments	**0.0**		**0.0**		**0.0**
Liquid/Marketable Investments **(Biz Related)**					
Group Co. Investments **(Biz Related)**					
Group Co. Investments **(Not Biz Related)**					
Unquoted/Dead Investments (Non Biz Related)					
Current Assets:	81.6	42.4%	57.3	46.8%	39.0
Deferred Tax Asset					
Inventories	48.9	365.0%	10.5	-6.9%	11.3
Receivables / Debtors	10.8	-32.8%	16.1	-17.6%	19.5
Debtors > 6 months	1.5	0.0%	1.5	18.8%	1.3
Debtors < 6 months	9.3	-36.1%	14.6	-20.1%	18.3
Cash and Bank	0.9	244.3%	0.3	-73.8%	1.0
Loans & Advances	21.0	-31.0%	30.4	324.8%	7.2
Loans & Adv to directors/partners etc (ICDs)/Diversions					
Loans and Advances given to others **(Biz Related)**	21.0	-31.0%	30.4	324.8%	7.2
Misc Exp. (DRE+PreOp+Prelim+Acc P&...)					
ASSET - TOTAL	**175.8**	2.9%	**170.8**	44.9%	**117.9**

The main categories of the Balance Sheet are categorized as follows:

1. Share capital

The term capital refers to the total investment of the company in terms of money, and assets. It is also called as total wealth of the company. When the company is going to invest large amount of finance into the business, it is called as capital.

Authorized and issued share capital

When a company is formed the authorized share capital and the nominal value of its shares are written into the company's Memorandum of   Association. Both the authorized and issued share capital is shown in the company's accounts.

Authorized capital is the maximum number of shares can be issued.

There are a number of different types of share capital, which carry different levels of risk dependent upon where they would rank for distribution in the event of liquidation of the company. The types of share capital in ascending order of risk are:

- Preference (or non-equity) shares
- Ordinary shares

Preference shares

Preference shares earn a fixed rate of dividend, which is normally payable half-yearly, but preference shareholders have no right of legal redress against the directors of the company if they decide that no preference dividend should be paid. However, if no preference dividend is paid for an accounting period then no other share dividend can be declared for the accounting period concerned. Preference shares can include these following features:

- Cumulative – if a dividend is not paid on time it is deferred to be paid later rather than omitted. The preference dividend is then said to be in arrears and must be paid at some future time before any other share dividend can be declared and paid.
- Redeemable – the shares are repayable at their nominal value in a given year or when the company chooses within a given period.
- Participating – in addition   to any fixed dividend the   participating preference shareholders participate in an additional dividend, usually a proportion of any ordinary dividend declared.
- Convertible – shareholders have the option of converting their prefer- ence shares into ordinary shares within a given period of time (the conversion period).

Ordinary shares

Ordinary shares comprise the main part of the share capital of a company. Ordinary shareholders are entitled to vote at the company's general meet- ings, giving them a say in company decisions including appointment of directors. They are entitled to the profits of the company which remain after tax and preference dividends have been deducted.

Share details

Details of shares and debentures issued during the accounting period will be shown in the company's balance sheet.

Reduction of share capital

A company may reduce its share capital with court approval. It may reduce, or do away with completely, liability on any share capital not fully paid up, it may cancel any paid up shares which is unrepresented by available assets, and it may repay any paid up share capital which is in excess of its requirements.

Addition in share capital

Addition in share capital doesn't require any specific approval .But analyst should analysed source of addition & purpose of it.

2. Reserves

Reserves can arise in several ways:
- by the accumulation of profits, from trading and from the sale of assets,
- by the issue of shares at a premium, i.e. at more than their nominal value,
- by the issue of warrants,
- by the upward revaluation of assets,
- by the acquisition of assets at below their balance sheet value.

Reserves can be reduced by:
- losses,
- share issue and share redemption expenses,
- revaluation expenses,
- revaluation deficits,
- writing off of goodwill.

Types of reserves

Reserves include capital and revenue reserves. By law certain of these reserves are non-distributable, these are:

- Share premium account – When shares are issued at a premium over their nominal value, the premium element must be credited to the share premium account. The share premium account has to be shown separately on the balance sheet and may not be paid out to shareholders except on liquidation or under a capital reduction scheme.
- Capital redemption reserve – Shares may be redeemed or purchased by a company out of distributable profits or out of the proceeds of a new issue of shares. Where redemption or purchase is out of distributable profits an amount equal to the amount by which the company's share capital is diminished must be set aside by the company in a reserve called

the capital redemption reserve. This is shown separately under other reserves.

■ Revaluation reserve – The surplus (or shortfall) on the revaluation of assets should be credited (or debited) to a separate reserve, the revaluation reserve.

■ Other reserves – prohibited from distribution by the company's memorandum articles.

3. Borrowings
A company's borrowings will broadly fall into three categories:

■ Bank overdrafts/Cash Credit(i.e. working capital facilities)
■ Long term Loans from financial institutions.
■ Debentures and unsecured loan stock and bonds. These can be bought and sold in the same way as shares in a company, and can be held by the general public.

Limitations on borrowings
The amount that a company can borrow may be limited by several factors such as:

■ The company's borrowing powers as limited by its Articles of Association (the internal rules upon which the directors run the company). These cannot be altered except by gaining the approval of the company's shareholders at a general meeting.

■ Restrictions imposed by existing borrowings. Terms of existing loan agreements may preclude the company from borrowing further.

■ The lender's requirement for capital and income cover.

■ The lender's general opinion of the company and its overall borrowing position.

Banking facilities
There are three main methods by which a company can borrow money from a bank:

■ **Bank overdrafts/Cash Credit** are technically repayable upon demand by the bank and can leave the company vulnerable to increases in interest rates. However, they are a simple method by which to fund day-to-day working capital requirements and the balance overdrawn is shown under current liabilities in the company's balance sheet.

Bank overdrafts are shown under the current liabilities heading in the balance sheet, although this only tells us the outstanding balance and not the amount of the overdraft/CC facility granted by the company's bank.

Other working capital facilities

Bills of exchange(or bill discounting) are a funding instrument to finance the sale of goods when the seller or exporter wishes to obtain payment at the time the goods are dispatched and the buyer or importer wants to defer payment until the goods reach them, or later.

Pre shipment Credit/Post shipment credit is the facilities which are given to exporter only for meeting their working capital requirement.

■ **Bank loans** are shown n the balance sheet under two headings, one in current liabilities which shows the amount of principal due to be repaid under bank loans within the next 12 months and the balance under long-term liabilities which shows the amount due to be repaid after 12 months.

Descriptions of the terms under which each loan is repayable, the rates of interest applicable on each loan and whether they are secured or unsecured will be in the notes to the accounts

Analyst should understand the recently added loan & purpose of it and validate it. And it also cross verified with total interest charged under P&L account.

Note: Bank generally offers two type of limit-

a) Fund based limit –Under this facilities fund is received in the borrowers account like FBCC.OD, PCL, BD, PSCL, Export finance, term loan, asset based finance etc.

b) Non fund based limits-   It is basically fees based service like LC, BG, or any other type of guarantee etc.

4. Unsecured loan from partners/shareholders/ICD etc

Borrower may also take unsecured loan from partner/shareholder/ICD etc. Analyst should identified whether it is the interest bearing or not. If it is interest bearing then it should be treated as a loan in other case it should be treated as a quasi capital.

5. Current liabilities & provisions

Defferd tax liabilities /Assets

Defferd tax liabilities /Assets arises due to timing difference of some items between companies act & income tax act, like depreciation, prior period items etc.

Creditors

Creditors are those to whom the company owes money, e.g. suppliers of raw material, who have given the company a credit period in which to pay and are shown as liabilities in the balance sheet.

Various types of creditors

■ Trade creditors – suppliers to whom the company owes money i.e. those from who the company has purchased goods on credit terms. The size of the trade creditors' figure will reflect the extent to which suppliers are financing the company's business.

The formula for calculating creditor days is as follows:

Creditor days = Trade creditors/Sales (turn over) 365

It is useful to compare debtor and creditor days to see if there are any significant variations between them. For example, if the company's credit period is 30 days (it is paying its bills in a 30 day period), and it is giving 100 days credit this could produce serious cash flow problems or be indicative of deficiencies in the company's debt collection procedures and very possibly bad debts.

Debenture (secured) loans – when a company wishes to issue loan cap- ital it can offer the lender some specific security on the loan. If it does so the loan is called a debenture, or debenture stock.

- Bank loans and overdrafts.
- Payments received on account – e.g. deposits from customers paid in advance for work which the company is undertaking or will undertake.
- Bills of exchange payable – a way of raising short term capital for the company. A bill of exchange is used to finance the sale of goods when the seller wishes to obtain payment at the time the goods are despatched to the buyer, and the buyer wants to defer payment until the goods are received by him, or later. A bill of exchange payable in a company's creditors would indicate that the company has purchased goods and has accepted a bill of exchange acknowledging its debt to the supplier and promising to pay at some future time.

C) Other liabilities

Other liabilities include which is not included above like, expenses payable, TDS payable, advance from customers. Analyst should identify that there is no major changes in other liabilities in comparison to last years. If it is found then proper clarification should be taken.

5) Fixed assets

Fixed assets is the assets which is purchased for long-term use and are not likely to be converted quickly into cash such as land , building & equipment .

The Companies Act 1956 requires fixed assets to be set out in the balance sheet under three headings:

- Intangible fixed assets will include such items as patents and trade- marks; brand names; goodwill; concessions; and capitalized develop- ment costs.
- Goodwill is the amount by which the value of a business as a whole exceeds the balance sheet value of its individual assets less liabilities. It is normally only recognized in the accounts of a company when it acquires another business, and it relates to the amount that the purchasing company has paid for the company being purchased over and above its balance sheet value.
- Tangible fixed assets are assets with a long working life which have not been bought by the company for resale purposes in the ordinary course of their business, but for the purpose, directly or indirectly of revenue generation. They will include items such as machinery on which the company's product is made, land on which the head office or factories are based, buildings such as the offices and factories, and motor vehicles (Lorries, sales representatives, cars, etc.).

The Companies Act 1956 specifies the following treatment in relation to fixed assets in a company's balance sheet:

- Fixed assets may be shown on a historical cost basis (what it cost to purchase), at valuation, or at current cost.
- Land assets must be classified as either freehold, long leasehold (if over 50 years

unexpired), or short leaseholds.

- Where fixed assets are included on a historical cost basis, the figures for cost, provision for depreciation since acquisition, and the current study material value must be shown.
- where fixed assets are included at valuation the years and amounts of the valuations must be shown, along with the names of the values and the basis of valuation in notes to accounts& auditor's report.
- where fixed assets are included at valuation or at current cost, histor- ical cost details must also be disclosed.
- Details must be given of additions and disposals during the period.

If in fixed assets, plant & machinery is added then analyst should find the source of finance & impact on turnover. And it should be linked with depreciation. He should also find the % of various assets like Plant & machinery, Land & building, Furniture & fixtures in total fixed assets .He should also analyzed whether exiting P&M is sufficient for current turnover.

7) Investments
If company has surplus fund which can be invested for getting a return on it or any its sister.

Investments fall into two categories:

- Investment in subsidiary companies.
- Investment in associated undertakings.

Participating interests (these are interests held by the company on a long-term basis to secure a contribution to its activities by the exer- cise of control or influence over another party or parties). This would involve a holding of 20% or more of the shares of another institution. A participating interest becomes an interest in an associated under- taking if the company exercises a significant degree of influence over the operating and financial policy of the company in which it has a participating interest.
- Other investments. Share holdings in other companies which are none of the above, but which the company feels is a good investment for it and will bring a good return.

Analyst should analyze % of investment made in sister concern. There may be possibility that it has diverted its capital/fund by way of investment. In that case, it should be deducted from capital for all analysis purpose.

8) Current Assets
A) Debtors

Debtors (also known as accounts receivables) are a current assets and rep- resent amounts owed to the company. The Companies Act 1956 requires the company to split their debtors figure into the following categories:
- Trade debtors – debts owed to the company arising from sale of goods to customers of the company on credit terms.
- Amounts owed by group companies – these amounts will represent inter-group trading activities, i.e. sums owed to the company by its parent company, fellow subsidiaries or subsidiaries of its own.
- Amounts owed by companies and other institutions in which the com- pany has a participating interest (debts owed to the company by insti- tutions in which the company has a holding of 20% or more of that institution's shares).
- Other debtors – for example debts due to the company from the sale of fixed assets or investments.

■ Prepayments and accrued income – for example rent and rates paid by the company in advance.

In balance sheet figure of debtors shows under two categories i.e. less than & more than 6 months.

Unfortunately in some instances the company will grant credit to a customer only to find that payment is not forthcoming. The debt then becomes classified as a bad debt. When the company recognizes that a debt is bad, the debt is written off as a charge to the P/L account. The balance appearing as debtors in the accounts will be reduced by the amount of the bad debt, and bad debts will be shown as an expense (which will only be shown separately in the accounts if the amount involved is material).

Companies have different debtor profiles

Supermarket chains will have very little showing in their accounts in the way of debtors, as most of their sales will be for cash, any debtors shown in their accounts are likely to be non-trade or prepayments. Other com- panies in contrast may conduct most or all of their trade on credit terms and will have large debtor balances.

Trade debtors/turnover

It is interesting to be able to look at a company's credit control policy. This can be done by using the Trade debtors/Turnover ratio (measuring this in terms of time), and then comparing this ratio to that of other com- panies in a similar industry:

Debt collection period (in days) Trade debtors/Sales (turnover) $\times$ 365

In a seasonal business it may be more accurate to calculate the debtor collection period on a monthly basis, but this would require monthly figures for trade debtors and turnover and knowing the seasonality of the company under review. This would require information beyond that required by law. For example:

Analyst should analyze the following points by debtor list:

■ Customer concentration – Is there too much reliance on one customer, or on one major industry? What would be the consequences to the company if they were to lose a major client?

■ What is the age pattern of the debtors? – Are some very old debts?

■ Is there adequate provision for bad and doubtful debts?

■ What is the company's credit granting policy?

B) Stock (Inventory) and work in progress

Stock (Inventories)

While companies have traditionally shown stocks as a single figure under current assets (described as 'stocks' or 'inventories' or 'stocks and works in progress). As per company's act 1956, stocks to be analyzed under the following sub-headings:

■ *Raw materials & consumables*: these are materials, components, or consumables (such as paint and oil) used in the making of a product.

■ Work *in progress*: these are partially complete items in the process of being turned from raw materials into the finished product (partially completed cars for example).

■ *Finished goods*: Finished goods and goods purchased for resale.

Valuing stock

The accurate and consistent valuation of stock is crucially important to the company, because quite small variations can have a significant effect on the profits reported by the company.

Inventory valuation methods

There are a number of different methods used to put a value on stock, of which the following are examples of the most commonly used:

■ *First in first out (FIFO).* This method of stock pricing assumes for accounting purposes that the stock has been used in the order in which it had been received by the company. Therefore if there have been price rises the stock which has not been used will be likely to be that which was purchased by the company at the higher price and the stock can be valued accordingly.

■ *Average, or weighted average cost calculation (WACC).* Where a company receives a number of stock deliveries during an accounting period at dif- ferent prices, the average price, or weighted average price, will be used.

■ *Last in first out (LIFO).* This method of stock pricing assumes for accounting purposes that the stock has been used first which is last received by the company. Therefore if there have been price rises the stock which has not been used will be likely to be that which was purchased by the company at the higher price and the stock can be valued accordingly

Accounting and stocks

Accounting Standard-2, requires that the amount at which stock and work in progress are shown in the company's accounts should be the 'total of the lower of cost and net realizable value of the separate items of stock and work in progress or groups of similar items'.

The Companies Act and AS-2 both regard that work in progress and finished goods should be valued at the full cost of purchase of the constituent parts plus the cost of conversion (including fixed overheads)

Net realizable value of work in progress and finished goods

This is the actual or estimated selling price of the company's product (net of trade but before early payment discounts) less all further costs to completion of the product and all costs to be incurred in marketing, sell- ing, and distribution.

When stocks are held which are unlikely to be sold within the turnover period normal to the company (e.g. excess stocks) this results not only in delayed profits but also the risk that the products deteriorate or become obsolete. This factor will need to be taken into account when calculating net realizable value.

Other factors affecting net realizable value could include perishability of goods, the whims of fashion, and (if the goods are sold abroad) changes in exchange rate between the selling and purchasing countries.

C) Other current assets

Other current includes that not includes above like miscellaneous expenses , preliminary expenses, outstanding.

The P/L account

The P/L account is also one of the basic components of the company's report and accounts. It is a record of the trading activities of a company for a given period of time. This period is called the accounting period and is normally a year. The balance sheet is always drawn up on the last day of the company's accounting period.

The P/L account:
■ Compares revenue for the year against the COGS and other expenses disclosing the P/L made.
■ Measures the current performance of the business and shows turnover expenses.
■ Reveals the pre-tax P/L figure, which is an important pointer to overall efficiency of the company.

P/L account shows three things; how the profit (or loss) was earned, how much was taken in taxation, and what happened to the profit (or loss) after taxation was deducted.

After the operating profit figure the formats then add other income and deduct other charges to reach the pre-tax profits figure.

P&L ACCOUNT *(sample)*

PARTICULARS	AUDITED		AUDITED		AUDITED
	31-Mar-11	% Growth	31-Mar-10	% Growth	31-Mar-09
PROFIT & LOSS ACCOUNT	Rs. Lacs	#N/A	Rs. Lacs	#N/A	Rs. Lacs
Sales/Receipts	130.4	37.8%	94.6	-18.6%	116.2
Other Income (part of Business Income)	19.7	2094.3%	0.9		
Other Income (Non Business income)					
TOTAL INCOME	150.1	57.2%	95.5	-17.8%	116.2
Opening Stock	10.5	-6.9%	11.3	-33.8%	17.0
Purchases	121.1	83.5%	66.0	-16.2%	78.8
Closing Stock	48.9	365.0%	10.5	-6.9%	11.3
Manufacturing expenses	20.2	544.0%	3.1	-45.8%	5.8
Wages	6.6	22.6%	5.4	19.0%	4.5
COST OF SALES	109.5	45.5%	75.3	-20.6%	94.8
GROSS PROFIT (as per books)	40.6	100.9%	20.2	-5.6%	21.4
GROSS PROFIT (Excl. Non Business Income)	40.6	100.9%	20.2	-5.6%	21.4
Administrative Expenses + any other exps	5.2	44.1%	3.6	-37.2%	5.7
Selling & Distribution Expenses	0.6	24.7%	0.5	-53.0%	1.0
Depreciation	7.0	91.5%	3.7	150.1%	1.5
Interest to FI/Banks	13.7	64.1%	8.3	5.4%	7.9
Interest to Pvt/Outside Parties	0.0	-52.2%	0.1	-43.3%	0.1
Non cash exps written off (Prelim Exps/Def. Rev Exp.)					
Salary to Partner/Director	3.0	0.0%	3.0	0.0%	3.0
Interest Expenses paid to partners/director					
PROFIT BEFORE TAX (as per books)	11.1	955.8%	1.0	-51.1%	2.1
PROFIT BEFORE TAX (Excl Non Business Inc)	11.1	955.8%	1.0	-51.1%	2.1
Tax	0.2	-24.1%	0.3		
PAT (as per books)	10.9	1298.2%	0.8	-63.8%	2.1
PAT (Excl Non Business Income)	10.9	1298.2%	0.8	-63.8%	2.1
CASH PROFITS (Excl Non Business Income)	17.9	302.3%	4.5	23.1%	3.6
Actual Cash Profit (Excl Non Business income)	20.9	180.6%	7.5	12.7%	6.6
PBDIT (Excl Non Biz Income, Incl. Rem/Sal to Dir/Partners)	34.8	115.8%	16.1	10.1%	14.7

The main categories of the P/L statement are categorized as follows:

- Turnover of the company is the figure representing the total sales of goods and services made by the company (after deduction of trade dis- counts and before addition of Value Added Tax (VAT) and other sales based taxes) from its ordinary activities during the accounting period.

  Under the Companies Act 1956 the following information must also be given by the company relating to its turnover:

- If the company has carried on two or more classes of business dur- ing the year which in the directors' opinion differ substantially from each other, it should describe the classes of business and split out each business's turnover.
- Companies which have two or more classes of business or which operate in two or more different geographical markets to report separately each market's turnover, pre-tax profits, and net assets.

- Cost of Sales (opening stock purchases closing stock) are the costs directly attributable to sales of the company's goods and services. Other sales costs shown here may include wages, materials, and manufacturing overheads including depreciation of machinery.

- Distribution costs are the costs incurred in getting the goods to the customer.

- Administrative expenses are for example office expenses, directors' and auditors' fees.

- Gross profit is obtained by deducting cost of sales from turnover.

- Operating profit (or trading profit) is gross profit less operating costs.

- Extraordinary items are amounts outside normal activities of the busi- ness which are not expected to recur, for example the profit from sell- ing a fixed asset such as a piece of land.

- Profit for the financial year is partly allocated to shareholders in the form of a dividend and partly retained by the business to finance its continuing operations.

Depreciation

This is a measure of the loss of value of an asset due to use, the passage of time, and obsolescence (obsolescence is particularly a problem in the field of high technology such as computers and electronic equipment). This includes the amortization of fixed assets which have a pre-determined future life and the depletion of wasting assets.

Factors affecting the depreciation of an asset will include the original cost of the asset, the estimated life of the asset, the method of depreciation calculation used, and the likely residual value.

Depreciation methods

Depreciation methods include
- straight line,
- Reducing balance,

■Sum of digits method.

Straight line is the most commonly used method and involves the fol-lowing calculation:

(Cost residual value)/Expected useful life Study material value

Traditionally fixed assets are shown in the balance sheet at cost less aggregate depreciation to date – this is known as 'net study material value'. It should be noted that this is in no sense related to the present market value of the asset.

As per Companies Act requires that the following be shown separately in the P/L account or in the notes annexed:

■Directors' remuneration(including pension costs and other benefits).

■ Particulars of staff, their wages and salaries; social security costs and pension costs.

■ Auditors' remuneration (including expenses).

■ Hire of plant and machinery, if material.

■ Depreciation and diminution in value of fixed assets. To summarize, the P/L account performs three functions:

■ It shows how much profit has been earned by the company, and whether this is sufficient to cover the dividends and to provide for expansion of the business.

■ Explains how the reported balance of profit was computed.

■ Shows how the reported profit has been distributed and what has been retained.

Other Important documents

Other than financial statements we should take others documents like tax audit report, ITR etc for better understanding of credit worthiness of borrower:

1. Tax Audit Report: As per sec 44 AB of income tax act 1961, Every person,-
Carrying on business shall, if his <u>total sales, turnover or gross receipts</u>, as the case may be, in business exceed <u>60 lakh rupees</u> in any previous year; or
Carrying on profession shall, if his <u>gross receipts</u> in profession exceed <u>15 lakh rupees</u> in any previous year shall be required to audit its books of accounts.

Report of audit of accounts to be furnished u/s 44AB

The report of audit of the accounts of a person required to be furnished u/s 44AB shall,
A) case of a person who carries on business or profession and who is required by or under any other law to get his accounts audited, be in form 3CA;
B) In case of a person who carries on business or profession, but not being a person referred to in clause (A), be in form 3CB.
Both the forms (3CA/3CB) consist the auditor's expression of opinion and to the best of his information and according to the explanations given to him, the particulars given in the said Form No.3CD and the annexure thereto true and correct.

2) The particulars which are required to be furnished u/s 44AB shall be in Form no. 3CD.

Analyst can find the following major information from this report which can help in analysis

a) Profit sharing ratio or change there in, if any

b) Fixed asset schedule (*as depreciation rate is different*)

c) Payment of statutory dues like EPF, ESI, TDS, vat, custom, excise etc on due date

d) Payment & receipts to/From related parties

e) Delayed interest or Penal interest

f) Loan taken or squared up from related parties during FY

g) Quantitative information regarding purchased, sales, consumed & inventory of raw material, finished goods

2. Income tax return : As per income tax act, every person has to required to furnish its return within due date (individual : 31 July & Companies : 30 sep of relevant assessment year)

Analyst can find the net worth & sources of income of assessee on the basis of his tax return.

3. Various statutory Returns (like sales tax, vat, service tax, and excise): There are the various return filed to various laws like sales tax act, custom tax act, etc. By which analyst can authenticate the information like turnover, default of statutory dues etc .

Banking analysis:

Analysis of banking statement is the second most important part after financial statements. Majorly all business transactions is done through banks .By analysis of banking statement of borrower analyst can find the flow of receipts, liquidity position, authentication of customer & suppliers , growth in turnover etc. Bank statement can be obtained for six months or a year.

Following are the points can be analyzed from banking statements:

1. **Credit Summation:** Please count the credit summation. If it six months then it will be doubled & compare with the turnover.It should be more than 80% of turnover.
2. **Credit instances (number of times):** Please count the number of credits made to the bank account while doing the credit summation. Credit summation gives a confidence on the turnover of the borrower. Many times the credits are mere entries and are not related to transactions of business and so happen in bulk. Therefore no of credits when looked in the light of the business segment
3. **Inward check Return criteria:** Not more than 4% of the number of transactions. If the return is not on account of breach in OD / CC limit, the same need not be counted for IRC Criteria. if it exceeds 4% analyst should understand the reasons for the cheque returns.
4. **Outward cheque returns criteria:** not more than 6% of the number of transactions (For cases where multiple cheques are deposited through single slips, the criteria for number of transactions to be not more than 8% of the value of transactions).If the percentage exceeds the stipulated norms based on number of transactions, CM to take call based on the value of Returns – IRC not to be exceed 10.5% of the value of Debits and ORC not to be exceed 2.5% of the value of credits.
5. **Limit:** Limit is the working capital facility being enjoyed by the client from banks.

I. **Overutilization of Limit:** 25% unadvised excess over OD/CC limit permitted. However, excess should have been regularized at least once in last three months. Accounts with OD/CC limit can be excess of 25% of the limit provided there is a letter from the bankers specifically approving the temporary increase in the limit / sanction of adhoc limit.

II. **Drawing power:** Drawing power is the amount which the customer is allowed to utilize out of the total limits sanctioned to him. Normally it is sum of receivables of up to 90 days and 75% of current stock. However some banks may keep it in a different Proportion and can be obtained from the sanction letter of the bank.

6. **CIBIL and RBI Defaulters list:** Individual and Corporate level CIBIL check to be done for all the clients. The director's name to be checked with RBI defaulters list. The CIBIL check of the individual will provide a summary of all the borrowing of the client individual name. It will also give an idea about the total actual leverage which is not reflected in books or reflected as part of quasi equity in the financials.

7. **Corporate guarantee:** In case if prime borrower is not eligible for loan. Then there may be case where a corporate guarantee is available for support ng. In that case we have to analyze the corporate guarantor on the basis of same parameter individually & jointly.

Cash flow statements

Cash is the 'lifeblood' of a business, and the company will only be able to survive if it is able to generate sufficient cash inflows to cover its cash outflows.

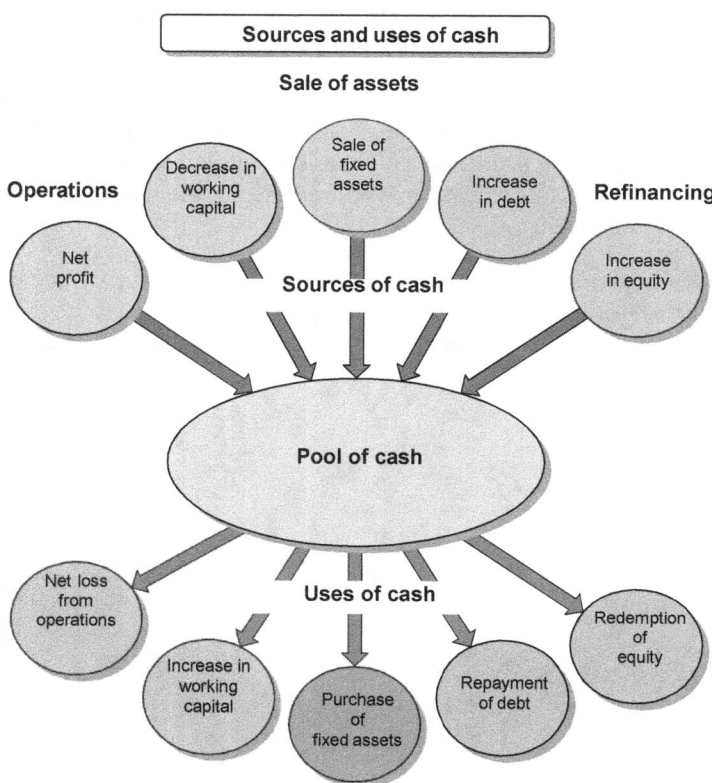

Companies can be profitable with negative cash flows and loss making with positive cash flows. A company can report a large profit for a year in which the cash balance may have fallen, perhaps as a result of heavy expenditure on fixed assets. Likewise, a company can be losing money and generating cash via asset disposals. It is important to understand that cash and profit are different.

The purposes of the cash flow statement are, therefore, to report the net change in the cash balance and to help explain how the surplus or deficit in cash arose.

A definition of cash is 'Cash in hand and deposits repayable on demand with any bank or other financial institution (this includes foreign currencies)'. Cash equivalents are 'short term, highly liquid investments which are readiy convertible into known amounts of cash without notice and which were within 3 months of maturity when acquired', this also includes foreign currencies.

It is important to realize that a company can be profitable and have a short- fall of cash, likewise a company can be losing money but have a surplus of cash. This can be summarized as follows:
▪ Increases in assets and decreases in liabilities represent an outflow of funds.
▪ Decreases in assets and increases in liabilities represent an inflow of funds. AS-3, issued by ICAI sets out a clear format for the cash flow statement, it should list the inflows and outflows of cash and cash equivalents for the accounting period, classified under the following three headings (and in the same order):

1. Cash flow from operating activities
2. Cash flow from investing activities
3. Cash flow from financing activities

CASH FLOW STATEMENT *(sample)*

CASH FLOW FROM OPERATING ACTIVITIES			
Net Profit Before Tax	**11.08**	**1.05**	**2.15**
Adjustments for:			
Depreciation	7.04	3.68	1.47
Non cash exps written off (Prelim Exps/Def. Rev Exp.)	-3.21	-1.94	0.00
Interest & Finance Charges	13.70	8.41	8.04
Non Business Income (Dividend, Interest on FD,etc.)	0.00	0.00	0.00
Operating Profit before Working Capital Changes	**28.62**	**11.20**	**11.66**
Adjustments for:			
Decrease/(Increase) in Receivables	5.28	3.44	-19.55
Decrease/(Increase) in Inventories	-38.35	0.78	-11.29
Decrease/(Increase) in Other Asset Deferred tax	0.00	0.00	0.00
Decrease/(Increase) in Misc. Exps.	0.00	0.00	0.00
Increase/(Decrease) in Payables	-7.42	10.08	35.28
Increase/(Decrease) in Deferred tax liability	-0.10	0.22	0.00
Cash generated from operations	**-11.97**	**25.72**	**16.10**
Income Tax paid	0.21	0.27	0.00
Net Cash flow from Operating activities	**-12.17**	**25.45**	**16.10**
CASH FLOW FROM INVESTING ACTIVITIES			
Sale / (Purchase) of Fixed Assets	15.49	-36.46	-80.32
Investments not related to business	0.00	0.00	0.00
Investments related to Business	0.00	0.00	0.00
Increase in Advances & others	9.43	-23.23	-7.15
Non Business Income (Dividend, Interest on FD,etc.)	0.00	0.00	0.00
Net Cash used in Investing activities	**24.92**	**-59.69**	**-87.47**
CASH FLOW FROM FINANCING ACTIVITIES			
Increase (Decrease) in Long term Borrowings	-2.67	29.26	28.39
Increase (Decrease) in Networth	0.19	-0.04	10.91
Increase (Decrease) in Funds from partners / directors	4.09	12.68	41.14
Interest paid	-13.70	-8.41	-8.04
Net Cash used in financing activities	**-12.09**	**33.49**	**72.39**
Net increase in cash & Cash Equivalents	0.65	-0.75	1.02
Cash and Cash equivalents as at 01.04.....	0.27	1.02	0.00
Cash and Cash equivalents as at 31.03......	0.92	0.27	1.02
Balance should become Zero	0.00	0.00	0.00
Cash & Cash Equivalents			
Cash in Hand			
Cash at Bank			
Cash & Cash equivalents as stated			

Ratio analysis

Financial statement analys s describes how to start this process and ratio analysis shows ways of continuing it. In recent years, ratio analysis has been eclipsed by cash-flow analysis.

A ratio is simply a means of highlighting, in arithmetic terms, the relation- ship between two figures (it is only useful if a significant relationship exists between the two figures). If the first figure (the numerator) is divided by the second (the denominator), a ratio is derived which can be expressed as a number in the mathematical notation for a ratio, or as a percentage.

Ratio analysis however has also evolved and also has its uses. It can help in analysing trends by comparing year on year statistics. A minimum of 3 years' accounts should be used. Ratio analysis moreover and has direct relevance to three areas of banking:

- Ratio analysis can provide useful clues as to the state of a company's health. Various mathematical models have been constructed in which a large number of ratios are compared and given different weightings to produce an overall credit score. Although there is a tendency here to quantify risks that are in part subjective, the credit score is a significant advance or reliance on one or two simple ratios.
- Ratio analysis can help in assessing a company's profitability and financial structure vis-à-vis its competitors via peer group analysis – an analytical technique comparing the financial ratios of one company against competitors in a similar industry sector (peers). While this approach has a tendency to generalize, it enables the identification of anomalies pertaining to a specific entity or industry sector.

The users

The purpose of financial statements is to provide information about a company's performance and financial standing. Many different parties have an interest in this information:

- Shareholders are interested in maintenance and growth of profits and dividends.
- Management is interested in the effective use of resources and future growth.
- Employees and trade unions are interested in profit and wages.
- Tax authorities are interested in collecting VAT (on sales) and corpor- ation tax (on profits).
- Trade suppliers are interested in solvency and short-term credit- worthiness.
- Customers wish to assess the risk of not being supplied.
- Bankers are interested in solvency, creditworthiness, debt levels, and the value of security.

Each user group will focus on different aspects of a company's business and will be looking at information from different sources.

It should be stressed that there is no 'standard set' of ratios, and there is no particular method of calculating ratios. The importance of specific ratios will vary from company to company (e.g the rate of stock turnover is important to a wholesaler but not to an advertising agency) and from user to user (e.g. the purpose of the credit facility).

The selection of and calculation of ratios is at the analyst's discretion. Depending on the nature of the company and lending risk, the analyst may only be interested in four or five of these ratios and the others may be irrelevant.

Some analysts have asked what are the proper ratios to use in an analysis and how do you calculate them. The answer to that is what is the nature of the company and what risks are you trying to analyse? Indeed one could calculate ratios on any facet of the company for example, the num- ber of employees per building, the number of employees per square foot of office space, the number of company cars per building, the ratio of cars to employees, etc. Ratios are merely a technique, it is for the analyst to understand the nature of the company and the lending risks and to select and calculate the ratios accordingly.

Classifying ratios

We will now consider a detailed ratio analysis of a set of financial statements. Whilst specific ratios relate to each statement, it is more useful to consider ratio analysis within the framework of their objectives. In other words, financial ratios exist to measure:

■**Performance -** The performance ratios we have been looking at give an indication of how well a company is controlling expenses and managing assets to produce sales and profit. Each ratio compared either two items from the P/L statement or an item from the P/L with one from the balance sheet. These are important considerations in helping establish whether the company is moving towards greater or lesser profitability. These are important considerations in helping establish whether the company is moving towards greater or lesser profitability.

■**Financial standing** - Financial standing ratios therefore are primarily balance sheet oriented and examine levels of debt in relation to both assets and other equity. Although they are to some extent indicators of ability to repay debt, it should be remembered that they do not give direct information. They tell you more about what would be left if a company were to stop trading at the date of the balance sheet than about the availability of cash to make regular interest payments.

■ **Return on investment-** These ratios relate to specifically to shareholders, particularly investors on the stock market. Several different ratios are used to measure the performance of the investment & to assess the likely future performance.

Broadly it can be classified into four categories:
■ Liquidity measurement Ratios
■ Asset management Ratios
■ Long term solvency measurement Ratios
■ Profitability measurement Ratios.

This is indeed a correct observation. The above four ratio categories are of concern to financial analysts looking at the financial condition of the company from a lending viewpoint and in effect form a subset of a larger set of ratios.

We will explain these categories in more detail below.

1. Asset management ratio

It also referred to as Activity or turnover Ratios. It:

➢ Deals with company's Operational Efficiency
➢ Measures how efficiently the assets are utilized
➢ Indicate the speed with which assets are being converted into sales

a) Stock Turnover ratio

Stock turnover = Cost of sales/Stock

A high stock turnover figure means a rapid rate of sale for stock and hence higher profits.

An alternative way of expressing the stock turnover ratio is as the num- ber of days' stock in hand.

Days' stock outstanding   Stock x   365/Cost of sales

Care should be taken with the stock figure since it may vary appreciably over time subject to production methods, the need to avoid raw material shortages and the need to hold higher levels of finished goods to support a major sales initiative. The breakdown of stock into raw materials, work in progress, and finished goods is normally available and the ratio for each category should be calculated to identify any major changes such as seasonal variations or slowdowns in delivery. It is also important when comparing different companies to ensure that stock is valued on a comparable basis, e.g. including, or excluding overheads, or on a first in first out (FIFO); last in, first out (LIFO) basis.

b) Debtor Turnover ratio

The debtor ratio can be expressed as the number of days' sales outstanding or the average collection period:

Days' debtors outstanding = Debtors x365/Sales

Care should be taken as the debtors outstanding will vary over time. A long collection period normally implies poor credit control procedures. Equally, one major debtor can have a disproportionate effect on this ratio, depending on their payment terms.

This is why it is useful when analysing a company to ask it for a list of its

10 largest debtors to see if they are evenly distributed or whether there are any disproportionately large clients.

C) Creditor turnover ratio

The creditors' ratio, which indicates how long the company takes to pay its suppliers, can be expressed as the number of days' purchases out- standing or average payment period.

Days' creditors outstanding   = Creditors x 365/Cost of sales

This ratio illustrates how adept the company is in using supplier credit.

2. Liquidity measurements ratio

The two key ratios normally calculated are the current ratio and the quick ratio.
Current ratio = Current assets/Current liabilities

The current ratio is used to compare assets which will be realized into cash as part of the company's normal working capital cycle with liabilities which should be paid during that cycle.
depending on the amount of stock that has to be held and the terms of trade. These factors are to a large extent fixed by market conditions, but will vary according to the amount of cash or short-term debt a particular company is carrying.

Practice will enable you to understand terms of trade, production cycles, seasonal requirements, etc., and how this translates into an acceptable ratio for a particular company in a specific industry sector.

3. Longer-term solvency measurement
To assess a company's longer range solvency, three ratios are commonly used:
- Leverage ratio(TOL/TNW)
- Gearing ratio (Debt/Equity)
- Interest cover ratio

4. Debt service coverage ratio

5. Debt income ratio

Indirectly, each is a measure of a company's ability to raise additional capital in the future, whether via additional bank debt or by the issue of new share capital.

a)   **Leverage ratio (TOL/TNW)=**   Total liabilities (including both long term and current)/ Shareholders' funds

Total liabilities = long term loan + Creditors,

Shareholders fund = Capital + own unsecured loan +R&S

 Leverage depends on the nature of a company's activities and is typically   in   the range of one or two times. It shows the relative contribution of total liability and owners in the total fund. The lower the TOL/TNW ratio, the higher the degree of protection.TOL/TNW below 4 is considered as satisfactory

b) Gearing ratio (Debt/Equity ratio) = Total interest bearing   debt/Shareholders' funds
It shows the relative contribution of Debt and owners in the total fund. A ratio in excess of 1:1 is normally considered to be excessive for production companies. Service and distribution companies can typically have more debt, as their assets are of a more liquid and seasonal nature for which short-term finance is more appropriate.

A high gearing ratio implies a higher financial risk, but can be tolerated if the profitability of a company is high, is relatively consistent and is a good generator of cash. A lower level of gearing is therefore appropriate, or measures should be taken to reduce the interest rate risk via financial instruments, or the conversion of a certain amount of debt into fixed rate borrowings.

b) **Interest service coverage ratio:** Earnings before interest and tax(EBIT)/Interest payments

This ratio, which is derived from the P/L account, demonstrates the amount of cover available before interest payments might be jeopardy ized.

▸　　　　This ratio is widely used by lenders to assess a firm's debt capacity
▸　　　　Higher the ratio better is the firm's ability to meet its interest burden
▸　　　　Lower ratio indicates excessive use of debt or inefficient operations

c) Debt service coverage ratio = EBDIT/Annual principal +interest

EBDIT = Earnings after tax+ Dep+ other non cash exp+ int on loan
The debt service coverage ratio (DSCR) is a financial ratio that measures the company's ability to pay their debts. In broad terms the debt service coverage ratio is defined as the cash flow of the company divided by the total debt service

▸　It is used by term-lending financial institutions
▸　Financial institution calculate the average debt service coverage ratio for the period during which the term loan for the project is repayable
▸　Debt service coverage ratio of 1.5 to 2.0 is considered as satisfactory

d) Debt Income ratio = Annual EMI burden/ Imputed Income x 100
　　　　　　　　　　　Imputed income =Income x Imputed margin
It compares an debt payments to the income generates. This measure is important in the lending industry as it gives lenders an idea of how likely it is that the borrower will repay the loan.

a)　Profitability measurement ratio

b)　Gross profit ratio= Gross profit/Turnover x 100

The gross profit margin looks at cost of goods sold as a percentage of sales. This ratio looks at how well a company controls the cost of its inventory and the manufacturing of its products and subsequently passes on the costs to its customers. The larger the gross profit margin, the better for the company.

c)　Net profit ratio = Net profit/Turnover x 100
The net profit margin measures profitability after consideration of all expenses including taxes, interest, and depreciation. It also shows the earning left for shareholders (owners) as percentage of turnover.

EBIDTA ratio = EBIDTA/Turnover x 100
(EBIDTA = Earnings after tax +Dep+ Interest+ Amortization + Tax)

An approximate measure of a company's operating cash flow based on data from the company's income statement. This earnings measure is of particular interest in cases where companies have large amounts of fixed assets which are subject heavy depreciation charges (such as manufacturing companies) or in the case where a company has a large amount of acquired intangible assets on its booksand is thus subject to large amortization charges (such as a company that has purchased

a brand or a company that has recently made a large acquisition). It is a good way of comparing companies within and across industries. Sometimes also called EBITDA or operational cash flow.
Others important ratio can be calculated

1. *ROCE (Return on Capital Employed)*

   This is the precise measure of a company's performance and is defined as:

   ROCE = Earnings before interest and tax/Capital employed
   Capital employed represents the total funds invested in the company shareholders' funds, long-term debt, which equates to net assets.

   ROE (Return on Equity)
   A shareholder is more interested in the return on shareholders' funds (or equity and reserves) after all the interest has been paid. The analyst is also interested, since this ratio demonstrates that acceptable performance is being achieved after taking into account the cost of debt.
   ROE = Earnings after tax/Shareholders' funds

   RATIO ANALYSIS *(sample)*

Growth Ratios :- Growth in Sales	37.81%	-18.59%	
Growth in Net Profits (PAT)	1298.24%	-63.77%	
Profitability Ratios :- Gross Profit Margin Ratio	31.13%	21.35%	18.40%
Net Profit Margin Ratio	8.34%	0.82%	1.85%
Cash Profit Ratio	13.75%	4.71%	3.11%
Leverage Ratios :- Debt Equity Ratio	0.68	0.87	0.54
Interest Coverage Ratio	2.54	1.92	1.82
DSCR	1.73	1.09	1.45
DSCR after the proposed Loan	0.87	0.46	0.486
TOL / TNW	1.0	1.456	1.085
Current Ratio	1.33	0.81	0.74
Working Capital Cycle :- Debtor Days	30.33	62.16	61.41
Stock Days	162.82	50.94	43.46
Creditor Days	82.75	187.15	111.92
Net Working Capital Cycle	110.41	(74.05)	(7.05)
	-89.283	-73.451	

Important points before interpreting the ratio

Analysts should therefore understand how this information is compiled, classified, and how the ratios are calculated (since many ratios are bespoke, there is no 'proper' ratio or 'proper way' to calculate a ratio), not only for the sake of due diligence in their profession but also because the number of financial scandals and corrupted financial statements signed off by unscrupulous or unprofessional auditors means that these databases, precise as they may be, ultimately depend on (and may suffer from) the integrity of the audited statements from which the database is compiled.

Finally, a clear understanding of how the ratios are calculated is essential not only for financial analysis but for the later stages of proactive credit risk management (e.g. establishing and defining the financial ratio covenants incorporated in the loan agreement to enhance the bank's security mechanisms and protection). Each source of information has its pros and cons. It is therefore important to understand the nature of the information being used.

Limitations of ratio analysis

This chapter has outlined the most frequently used ratios in the analysis of financial statements. However, depending on the objective of the analyst, many more ratios can be calculated and used. Of course, not all ratios are relevant to each company being analysed. This depends on the individual circumstances of the company.

Ratio analysis mainly enables the analyst to structure his investigation. It is also useful in highlighting trends, but the limitations of the technique should always be borne in mind when interpreting the figures.

- Publicly available information is often not sufficiently detailed and frequently out of date.
- Each company may have adopted different accounting policies and adjustments must be made to make the figures comparable.
- The introduction of earnings before interest, taxation, depreciation, and amortization (EBITDA) is used by some analysts in an attempt to provide comparative data, which excludes some of the accounting policy differences. (Amortization is the writing off of intangibles, as depreciation is the writing off of tangible assets.)
- 'Window dressing' the balance sheet at year end is not uncommon.

Management manipulates the balance sheet for that day to show the company in a stronger position. This can be done by, for example, run- ning down stocks and drawing down long-term loans to demonstrate a more liquid working capital position.

- There should always be a logical relationship between the numerator and the denominator, which should both be measured consistently and on the same basis as any comparative ratio.

- When comparing ratios over time, it is important to remember the possible effects of inflation and general economic conditions which tend to be cyclical.
- When comparing one company's ratio to another's, the second company should be similar both in terms of industry sector, size, and technology.
- A ratio should always be interpreted in the full context of the com- pany's affairs, for example, a fall in sales by 1% would be a disaster if the market grew by 20%, but would be a real success if the market fell by 20%.

If the analyst takes these factors into account, although ratios will not always provide direct answers to every question about a company, they will, nevertheless, provide a useful insight into the company's affairs. Ratios tend not to provide answers, but raise further questions!

Working Capital Management Analysis

Meaning & Importance:

Every business needs funds for two purposes- for its establishment and to carry out its day to day operations. Long term funds are required to create production facilities through purchase of fixed assets such as plant and machinery, land, building, furniture etc. Investments in these assets represent that part of firm's capital which is blocked on a permanent or fixed basis and is called fixed capital.

Working capital is the life blood and nerve centre of a business. Just as circulation of blood is essential in the human body for maintaining life, working capital is very essential to maintain the smooth running of business. *No business can run successfully without an adequate amount of working capital.*

Working capital refers to that part of firm's capital which is required for financing short term or current assets such as cash, marketable securities, debtors, and inventories. In other words working capital is the amount of funds necessary to cover the cost of operating the enterprise.

Thus, Working capital means the funds (i.e.; capital) available and used for day to day operations (i.e.; working) of an enterprise. It consists broadly of that portion of assets of a business which are used in or related to its current operations. It refers to funds which are used during an accounting period to generate a current income of a type which is consistent with major purpose of a firm existence.

Determinants of Working Capital:

1. Small or Large Business

It is the first determinant of working capital that it is affected with the nature of business. Business may be small or large. In small business, company need high working capital because, small business is relating to trading of goods, for starting small business, you need very small fixed capital but need high working capital for paying day to day expenses. But in large business, we require more fixed capital than working capital for purchasing fixed asset.

2. Small or Large Demand

Nature of demand also absolutely affects the working capital need. Some product can be easily sold by businessman, in that business; you need small amount of working capital because your earned money from sale can easy fulfill the shortage of working capital. But, if demand is very less, it is required that you have to invest large amount of working capital because your all fixed expenses must be paid by you. For paying fixed capital you need working capital.

3. Production Policy

Production policy is also main determinant of working capital requirement. Different company may different production policy. Some companies stop or decrease the production level in off seasons, in that time, company may also reduce the number of employees or decrease the purchasing of new raw material, so, it will certainly decrease the amount of working capital but on the side, some company may continue their productions in off season, in that case, they need definitely large amount of working capital.

4. Credit Policy

Credit policy is relating to purchasing and selling of goods on credit basis. If company purchases all goods on credit and sells on cash basis or advance basis, then it is certainly company need very low amount of working capital. But if in company, goods are purchased on cash basis, and sold on credit basis, it means, our earned money will receive after sometime and we require large amount of working capital for continuing our business.

5. Dividend Policy

Dividend policy also effect working capital requirement. Company can distribute major part of net profit. But, if there is no reserve, we have to invest large amount in working capital because, lacking of reserve will affect on adversely on fulfill our liabilities. In that case, we have to yield working capital by taking short term loan for paying uncertain liability.

6. Working Capital Cycle

Working capital cycle shows all steps which starts from cash purchasing of raw material and then this converted into finished product, after this it is converted into sale, if it is credit sale, debtors will also the part of working capital cycle and when we gets money from our debtors, it is the final part of working capital cycle. If we receive fastly from our debtors, we need small amount working capital. Otherwise, for purchasing new raw material, we need more amount of working capital.

7. Manufacturing Cycle

Manufacturing cycle means the process of converting raw material into finished product. Long manufacturing cycle will create the situation in which we require large amount of working capital. Suppose, we have to construct the building, for constructing colony of buildings, it may consume the time more than 5 years, so according to this we need working capital.

8. Business Cycle

There is two main part of business cycle, one is boom and other is recession. In boom, we need high money or working capital for development of business but in recession, we need only low amount of working capital.

9. Price Level Changes

If there is increasing trend of products prices, we need to store high amount of working capital, because next time, it is precisely that we have to pay more for purchasing raw material or other service expenses. Inflation and deflation are two major factors which decide the next level of working capital in business.

10. Effect of External Business Environmental Factors

There are many external business environmental factors which affect the need of working capital like fiscal policy, monetary policy and bank policies and facilities.

Working Capital Concepts:

- **Gross Working Capital:** It means Current Assets.
Gross working capital = Current Assets
- **Net Concept:** It means difference between Currents Assets & Current Liabilities. This is knows as **Qualitative** aspect of Working Capital

Net working capital = Current Assets – Current liabilities

(Current Assets = Bills receivable, Short term loans , Sundry debtors, inventories, cash & banks , prepaid expense, accrued income)
(Current liabilities =bills payable, sundry creditors, dividend payable, outstanding expenses, bank overdraft)

Working capital Gap
Working capital gap shows inadequacy of working capital. It can be calculated by

Working capital Requirement *(a)*	= XXX
Less: Working capital facilities	= XXX
Available i.e. CC/OD/PSL/PSCL (b)	
Working capital Gap *(a-b)*	= XXX

Note: Working capital requirement can be calculated by tandon committee recommendation i.e. MPBF= 75% of Net working capital requirement.

Meaning of Operating Cycle/Working Capital Cycle:
- Cash ☐ Raw-Materials ☐ Work-in-Process ☐ Finished Goods ☐ Cash
 Working capital cycle = Debtor turnover ratio +inventory turnover ratio- creditor turnover ratio. E.g if debtor inventory ratio is 60 days, inventory turnover ratio is 30 days & creditor turnover ratio is 30 days.

Working capital cycle = 60 days +30 days -30 days = 60 days

The inadequate working capital has the following adverse consequences:
➤ It stagnates growth. It becomes difficult for the firm to undertake profitable projects for non-availability of working capital funds.
➤ It becomes difficult to implement operating plans and achieve the firm's profit target.
➤ Operating inefficiencies creep in when it becomes difficult even to meet day-to-day commitments.
➤ Fixed assets are not efficiently utilized for the lack of working capital funds. Thus the firm's profitability would deteriorate.
➤ Shortage of working capital funds renders the firm unable to avail attractive credit opportunities etc.
➤ The firm loses its reputation when it is not in a position to honor its short term obligations. As a result, the firm faces tight credit terms.
The excessive working capital is equally unprofitable. The extra working capital is not utilized in business operations and earns no profit for the firm. It results in unnecessary accumulation of inventories, leading to inventory mishandling, waste; theft etc. The abundance of working capital would lead to waste and inefficiency

So analyst should develop very good understanding about working capital of the borrower.

Cash flow forecasting

Introduction

Cash Flow Forecasting is a subject which encompasses a broad range of financial and technical techniques which lead ultimately to assessing a future scenario of a company's financial condition.

Here, we briefly raise the subject within the contest of Credit Risk Management in order to note the underlying assumptions and techniques used to project financial statements in the future, and place it in the overall banking context:

- the different underlying rationales and uses of forecasts,
- underlying assumptions of forecasts,
- how to use these financial projections and run sensitivity analyses.

Why make such projections 4, 5, or more years into the future? The simple answer is that banks /NBFC need to look as far ahead as they have committed themselves, especially in a term lending situation.

Financial statement forecasting framework

Financial forecasting requires skills which build on the financial analysis chapters described earlier. Essentially, these factors include:

- Projecting the P/L statement using key assumptions.
- Projecting the balance sheet using elements derived from the P/L statement.
- Estimating new money needs and interest coverage ratios from the projected statements.

The nature of term lending

Typically a term loan is for 5–7 years and is raised to purchase assets such as plant or equipment. These assets are expected to produce other assets which, when converted to cash through completion of the manufacturing process and sale, will contribute to repayments. The fixed asset being financed is not itself expected to repay the loan.

Hence, banks/NBFC involved in term lending or acquisition financing will be concerned about the company's future operations because it is these that will provide the cash flow for debt servicing and repayment.

Projections aim to look ahead and identify potential problems. You may then decide that the lending opportunity is inappropriate or needs to be reconfigured before committing to participation. Projections can also identify potential future difficulties as well as the way to possible solutions, such as drafting of loan covenants or reconfiguring loan repayment schedules. Finally, sensitivity analysis in which key variables are modified in order to gauge the company's 'sensitivity' to change may provide clues as to the potential difficulties facing a company's debt repayment commitments.

Financial projections

Hence the focus on financial statement projections. Basically, the source of repayment for a term loan, like any other loan, is cash, and a proper analysis should assess the borrower's ability to service existing and future debt commitments by generating cash from future business operations.

Some of the questions that can be answered using projected financial statements are:

- Will the firm be able to pay back its current debt obligations out of future earnings?
- How much can sales revenues, profit margins, and cash flow shrink before payback is in jeopardy?
- How much new debt will the firm need to support its future growth?
- How much new debt can the company take on and service from earnings after having satisfied other needs such as working capital, plant expenditures, etc.?
- Does the company's new debt need mean that the company's future financial structure will be satisfactory or too highly geared or leveraged?
- Does the loan have an appropriate and specific reason (project finance, expansion, acquisition, and debt refinancing) or is it non-specific (a danger signal)?
- What kind of repayment schedule should be set up for the new debt?
- What forms of protection and control need to be included in the loan agreement to afford maximum safety for the lender"s money?

Projections are not intended to predict the future but rather are a tool to enhance understanding of a company. However, as with any analytical technique, projections should not be used on their own but also in conjunction with the other techniques outlined in this study material.

Uses of cash flow forecasts

Cash flow forecasts have numerous applications which are referred to elsewhere in this series. Here we note that cash flow forecasts can be used to

- Assess the long-term risks in a lending situation.
- Test the assumptions of a given project.
- Understand the parameters in a project in order to devise appropriate security structures and financial ratio covenants in the loan agreement.

Analyzing the spreadsheets (Credit Appraisal Tools)

Now we have developed very good understanding about the financial statements.

But account presentations vary considerably from country to country, company to company, and even from year to year. Company may present its financial statements in horizontal or vertical form

Analysis is therefore easier when the company accounts are reclassified into a standardized format that avoids distortions and is familiar to the credit analyst. Such standardized formats enable comparison with   competitors and industry sectors

Once the company's financial statements have been spread, the task of analyzing the information in them can begin. There are several approaches that can be adopted in a financial analysis of the spreadsheet. It is important that the analyst has at least three, and ideally five years, of financial information available to enable identification of trends over time. Much of the work in credit analysis consists of asking the right questions. The analyst should therefore be thinking about and analyzing the numbers on the spreadsheet and asking questions such as:

- Analyst can analyze trend analysis by spreadsheet. Debt, stock, share capitals, net worth, and sales all need to be considered as trends. This is one of the primary techniques in credit analysis. He should analyze whether trend of same is increasing or decreasing.
- Is the stock too high, debtors too low?
Is there any business segment is added
- Is all the expenses is increased or decreased in proportionate to its turnover. If there is any abnormal changes.
- Is the company progressing or regressing in its areas of activity?
- Are changes in various figures adequately explained in the annual report? What are their causes?
- Financial ratios can also be compared to those of previous years in trend analysis, or against major competitors.
In this way you can establish whether the company has a policy of ploughing back profits into retained earnings and investing them in the company, or paying them out as dividends.
Analyst can also assess how much fund can give to borrower against his proposals.
In assessing financial risk, t is important not just to look at the numbers, but to tie them into additional factors which could be affecting them. These will include: where the company operates, recent alliances, changes in management, ownership, operations, or the regulatory environment.

Such factors will not appear in the statements but will have a definite impact on the operations of the company, and even on its ability to remain a viable creditworthy entity in the future, for example, over the period of a long-term financing facility.

6 Transaction Risk

Once the borrower (financial and Non-financial) risk analysis is completed; the facility structure needs to be set in place appropriately (in light of the borrower's condition). This is known as the transaction risk.

Most businesses need to borrow money, and obtaining a loan from a bank/NBFC is the most usual way of financing a business. If successful in an application for a loan, an individual, partnership, or company has to enter into a loan agreement that sets out the terms on which the loan is given. A loan agreement is entered into by the bank/NBFC as lender, and by the individual, partnership, or company that borrows as borrower. A loan agreement contains all the terms and conditions under which the lender will lend the borrower the money. It states the amount of the loan, when the amount will be lent, the tranches if the money is to be lent in amounts at different dates, the repayment schedule, the interest to be paid by the borrower, and other conditions, terms, and warranties required by the lender from the borrower.

Term loan agreements

The loan agreement is the legal document that defines the relationship between the borrower and the lender. Understanding this document is critical to understanding the legal relationship between the various parties.

The loan agreement should give the lender the right to terminate the loan agreement if any of the following events occur:

- non-payment of principal,
- non-payment of interest,
- acceleration of other indebtedness (cross-default),
- voluntary or involuntary bankruptcy.

These events are known as '**events of default**' and the mechanisms in the loan agreement used to control them are known as loan agreement covenants.

Covenants, events of default, and protection

The issues of protection and control deserve mention. In term lending, the bank expects its primary source of repayment to be operating cash flow. Industry analysis on problem credits has revealed that there are several warning signals pointing to a company's ability or inability to generate sufficient cash flow (either internally or externally) to meet its needs and ensure its solvency.

They include:

- inadequate working capital;
- a sharp fall in the company's share price, reflecting the market's per- ception of the company's future cash flow;
- low or negative retained earnings in relation to assets;
- an unexpected change in 'corporate objectives', management structure or business profile', such as the introduction of new products or divisions;

- vulnerability to economic cycles from debt-heavy balance sheets or high fixed-cost operations;
- debt repayment schedules inappropriate in relation to cash flow.

Hence, it is important when drafting loan agreements, and more specifically covenants, to have undertaken a financial analysis of the borrower beforehand so that the ratios and clauses incorporated have some relevance and effectiveness with respect to the borrower's particular circumstances (e.g. industry peer ratios). It will be necessary to test the covenants which have been included in the loan agreement and see how they hold up against various financial projections (e.g. baseline, upside, downside). This is important because, in the event of declining financial strength, the proposed covenants will enable the bank to take action to protect its loan before it becomes too late to arrest the borrower's financial deterioration. And it should also include the financial covenants which are designed to preserve and control the firm's cash flow and its financial strength

It may be categorized into two type:

Primary covenants

Primary covenants relate directly to the company's financial structure.
Financial covenants can include:
- limitation of future debt (including contingent liabilities);
- prohibition of new secured debt or obligations which will rank ahead of the proposed term loan ('negative pledge');
- provision for a minimum level of working capital;
- provision for a minimum level of net worth.

Such limits can either be defined in absolute or ratio terms.

Secondary covenants

Secondary covenants relate to the company's management and ongoing operations. These can include:
- prohibitions on the sale of subsidiaries or assets;
- limitations on the prepayment of other debt;
- prohibitions on mergers or consolidations without consent of the lenders;
- limitations on investments or capital expenditures;

Indeed, some companies may resist the inclusion of financial covenants. From the lender's point of view, covenants should be designed to preserve upside potential and protect against downside risk. You should use your projections to see whether the covenants will enable the banks to adopt corrective or protective action before it becomes too late to stop the company's financial deterioration.

Events of default

Events of default are conditions under which the lending bank can call in the loan for prepayment. This right to accelerate is rarely used. Rather, this covenant strengthens the hand of the bank during negotiations to restructure the loan or take steps to protect its position.

Events of default can either be temporary breaches (technical defaults) such as failure to meet a ratio requirement or financial default (failure to meet an interest payment). In such cases, waivers are typically requested from (and granted by) the lender. The important thing to remember is that you, as the lender, must always inform the borrower, in writing, that you are aware of the breach and agree to its waiver (if in fact you choose to do so). If the breach is not acknowledged and formally addressed, you may have difficulty later in enforcing your legal right of acceleration when the event of default occurs again.

Follow-up on loan agreement compliance

Following up on compliance with loan agreements is important but is nevertheless neglected by some lenders. This is extremely dangerous because events of default can go by with the banks failing to notify the borrower. When the banks decide later to call in the loan, the borrower can oppose this claiming that non-notification of the event of default constituted a 'tacit approval'. So it is important to understand loan covenants and monitor the loan agreement!

A checklist of items to review compliance is valuable. Such a checklist eliminates the need for the loan agreement to be read again every time a statement is received from the borrower. The checklist, for example, can include the lists of documents to be received and at what intervals.

Steps to be taken after default

Disputes between parties in the commercial finance setting often involve lending and rate formulas, interpretation of loan agreement covenants, bankruptcy law, asset valuation issues, balance sheet, and other financial analysis.
Rarely, while the ongoing lending relationship exists, will these disputes ripen into discrete litigation. These disputes may be resolved quickly by agreement because of the exigencies of the situation, or simply by the passage of time because of the inability of one party under applicable law to force the other party to perform.
For example, if the borrower wants to draw down on a line of credit, and the lender refuses because the lending formula and financial ratios under the loan agreement allow it to decline to lend, the parties may agree on what to do. If they do not agree, the lender simply will not lend at that time. It will all happen quickly because of pressing business issues; neither party will look to a court to resolve the immediate problem.

However, litigation may arise out of the dispute. The lender may decide to call a default and demand repayment of the loan because of the borrower's failure to maintain the collateral and financial ratios, or other breaches of the loan documents. The borrower may respond with a claim for damages due to the lender's failure to lend, and assert defences to the lender's claims. When this happens, the lending relationship is over and litigation becomes the focal point of their relationship.

Lenders rely on specific legal remedies designed to recover the loan, and preserve, foreclose and liquidate collateral. The law allows a lender to take speedy action to protect, preserve or liquidate its collateral position.
Similarly, borrowers rely on the specific protections available under applicable

debtor/creditor laws to protect their rights. Thus, a borrower can take speedy action, to the extent allowed by law, to try to prevent the lender from exercising remedies that could impair the borrower's continued operation.

Neither party, however, can obtain an order of specific performance direct- ing a lender to lend or a borrower to perform its covenants under a loan agreement (other than those relating specifically to collateral preservation and maintenance).

Depending on the specific situation, the lender will decide whether to call a default and exercise its remedies, and the borrower will decide whether to defend against the exercise of remedies by the lender and/or assert a claim for damages against it.

7 Fraud Detection & Control

A) Instances of fraud: Fraud happens in many forms. In this section we are discussing the major financial frauds and methods of identifying them.

I. Tampering with financials

Where organizations prepare different financials for finance purpose, the same can be verified from CA website. The financials obtained from MCA website compared with those submitted to you will throw up differences if any.

II. Fake Income tax returns

Where organizations submit fraudulent income tax returns to INTEC showing higher income and/or tax paid, the same can be verified from the income tax department.

III. Fake and tampered bank statement

➤ Check the date of the statement properly on every page. The date should be continuous. Missing dates in between may mean that the statement has been photocopied and a few entries have been removed while photocopying.

➤ Bank statement should be stamped by the bank.

➤ Check credit summation and debit summation and verify it with the page total/month total figures.

IV. Fake CA stamp on audited financials

Check the membership number of the CA at www.icai.org. The details of the CA along with his address and whether he is in practice or not, is available at this website.

V. Fake quotation of equipment or procurement of second hand equipment with collaboration of equipment seller

This can be avoided to some extent by meeting suppliers.

B) Misrepresentation or suppression of facts in audited financial statements

I)   *Revenue related*
➤ Fictitious revenue
➤ Recording of goods or services that did not occur.
➤ Fake customers.
➤ Sales with conditions.
➤ Timing differences.
➤ Recording revenue and/or expenses in improper periods
➤ Shifts revenues or expenses between one period and the next, increasing or decreasing earnings as desired
➤ Inventory valuation
➤ Accounts receivable
➤ Business combinations

II)   **Assets** *related*
➤ Improper asset valuations
➤ Fixed assets
➤ Capitalized expenses

     III)   *Liabilities related*

- ➢ Concealed liabilities and expenses.
- ➢ Liability/expense omissions
- ➢ Failure to disclose warranty costs and liabilities
- ➢ Suppression of facts in respect of legal cases which can impact the company adversely.
- ➢ Liability omissions

III) ***Other disclosure***
- ➢ Improper disclosures
- ➢ Subsequent events
- ➢ Management fraud
- ➢ Related-party transactions
- ➢ Accounting changes
- ➢ Utilization of money for purposes other than desired by lender.

Ways to detect frauds in financial statements:

Check for Fictitious revenues and other details as described below:

I. Rapid growth or unusual profitability, especially compared to that of other companies in the same industry

II. Recurring negative cash flows from operations or an inability to generate cash flows from operations while reporting earnings and earnings growth

III. Significant transactions with related parties or special purpose entities, not in the ordinary course of business or where those entities are not audited.

IV. Unusual growth in the number of days' sales in receivables

V. An unusual surge in sales by a minority of units within a company, or of sales recorded by corporate headquarters

VI. Unusual growth in the number of days' sales in receivables

VII. Unusual decline in the number of days' purchases in accounts payable

VIII. Assets, liabilities, revenues, or expenses based on significant estimates that involve subjective judgments or uncertainties that are difficult to corroborate

IX. Unusual increase in gross margin or margin in excess of industry peers

X. Allowances for sales returns, warranty claims, and so on that are shrinking in percentage terms or are otherwise out of line with industry peers.

XI. Reducing accounts payable while competitors are stretching out payments to vendor

XII. Domination of management by a single person or small group (in a non owner managed business) without compensating controls

XIII. Significant related-party transactions not in the ordinary course of business or with related entities not audited

XIV. Significant bank accounts or subsidiary or branch operations in tax haven jurisdictions for which there appears to be no clear business justification

XV. Overly complex organizational structure involving unusual legal entities or managerial lines of Authority.

XVI. Known history of violations of securities laws or other laws and regulations, or claims against the entity, its senior management, or board members alleging fraud or violations of laws and regulations

XVII. Unusual change in the relationship between fixed assets and depreciation

XVIII. Adding to assets while competitors are reducing capital tied up in assets

8 Fourteen principals of Lending

1. Quality of credit is more important is more important than exploiting new opportunities-Put simply by a wise old banker, 'any fool can lend money, but it takes a lot of skill to get it back.'' You cannot charge a high enough interest rate to compensate for loans that are likely never to be repaid but in times of loan expansion, it is easy to seek to override this rule about credit quality .Such an attitude is just as dangerous as that of the businessman who is sales not profit oriented. In analyzing the degree of risk which a bank will assume in a credit, careful consideration should be given to the borrower's management experience, capabilities, policies, profitability, cash flow, and net worth. as a lending officer, you must decide for yourself how much money the borrower should borrow, how long it will take before repayment is complete , and the true purpose of a loan .

2. The character of the borrower or in the case of corporation the character, the principal management & shareholders –must be free of any doubt as to their integrity-If you should not approve the loan .You must, therefore, check on the moral standing and style of business before beginning negotiations. Remember that banks that associate with people of less than acceptable character damage their own reputation far beyond the profit obtained on the transaction.

3. If you do not understand the business model, do not lend to it -Successful banks specify precisely their terms of lending for appropriately differentiated risk assets, and they take pains to understand the market sectors in which they engage .the head of a lending group will decide what types of borrowers are acceptable and form of borrowing, amounts, periods security, documentation, and so on. But more important, the group head will understand he risk and return feature of each class of risk assets and, if necessary, employ specials or adequately experienced personnel before undertaking the business. After all, if you do not understand the industry or the sector, how can you evaluate the risks? Furthermore, customers will have respect only for the banks which take the trouble o understand their position.

4. It is your decision & you must feel comfortable with it according to your judgment-Credit decisions are personal. they cannot be made solely on the basis of guidelines or analytic techniques . Each lending officer must exercise common sense and good judgment. You must also be sure that it is your own independent judgment on each transaction and that you are not unduly influences by your associates. Remember that your NBFC, as a respected member of society, must act responsibility in evaluating risks, in negotiating terms, in competitive positions and in credit administration. In a decentralized credit procedure, group heads and other lending officers continue to bear responsibility for credit within their areas. During the 2007-08 recessions, the dangers of poor credit judgments shook many banks/investments banks to their roots. These lesson must be borne in mind whatever the phase of the cycle. The cost of loan losses is not just the write – off of the bad debt, it is also the cost of using talented human manage recovery situations. Our first principle could, in fact, be restated as follows: It takes a lot of good banker's time to clear up the mess of one bad decision. It is clear, then, that as a lending officer you must be comfortable with this decision because you will have to live with it.

5. If you have all the facts, you do not need to be a genius to make the right decision-Unlike the cat in the proverb, curiosity never killed a lending of. It pays to know. The more questions you ask, the more you understand the case. Also, the more respect you will gain in the end from borrowers who prefer o deal with a lender who understands their industry. Facts are helpful and, properly organized, will often make thedecision easy., Now we come to the second group of credit principles , which are related more directly to the borrower , rather than to the lender.

6. The business is inevitable i.e current market situation-simply stated like that , this does not seen to have much to do with credit . But as lenders , you must always be conscious of the current point in the business cycle so that you can evaluate the risky likely to arise when economics conditions change in the future . Things are always either getting better or getting worse, but sometimes the change is imperceptible. At certain points in the business cycle, ending appears less risky. It has been well said that bad loans are made in good times. Similarly, lending becomes more apparently dangerous in very bad economic conditions. In fact, banks that lend in bad times will, provided they have made a wise credit decision, gain permanent friends.

7. Although it is harder than evaluating financial statement, assessing a company's management quality is vital-Quality of management is displayed in many ways : the choice of an appropriate style for the industry (autocratic or democratic) , the ease or difficulty with which senior positions can be filled from outside the company , the style of the company's offices , the way in which innovation is treated , the reputation among competition . There are , of course , many other ways in which it shows :Do senior executives have a flamboyant life – style ? Are employees encouraged to own part of the company ?What are the feelings of frontline management ? Asking questions of others in the industry will also help you assess a company's management quality. If managers own the company or a major part , this may be in itself no comfort . They can bankrupt themselves just as easily as a professional management can bankrupt a company owned by holder.

8. Collateral security is not substitute for repayment, And where security is taken, a professional & impartial view of its value & market ability must be obtained - Repayment, as said before, comes from cashflow ; security is taken partly to prevent these assets from bring available to other lenders and partly to place the lender in a stronger negotiating position because the assests are usually necessary to operate the bus ness . When security is valued, there must be no conflicts of interest by the valuer . You must also be conscious of differences in market value. Such differences can sometimes be recognized by insisting on margins .That's, loan must be covered by, say, 150% in collateral security, valued at current market prices .

9. Lending is smaller is riskier than lending to larger ones. - Although the same principles apply to small firms as to large ones, in a smal firm managerial resources are fewer. In large firms, there can be many decision makers all running their own division or subsidiaries. In this way, there can b more jobs for good managers – and thus greater depth of management – than in a small firm.

10.Bamks should be participants in lending to borrowers . It is often a danger sign if local banks are not lenders to local firms. They may already know too much about the risks of such a credit. In the same way , be caution with those who seek to change to a new bank because they are dissatisfied with their present bank . New accounts, it has been said, go bad more often.

11. If a borrower wants a quick answer, It is "NO". - You into a lending decision should be told these principles. On the other it pays to be prepared for requests from borrowers. Indeed, the best is to be sure that officers seeking new business check out their targets of companies with their superior officers before visiting he companies.

12. If the loan is to be guaranteed, be sure that guarantors are served as well as the borrower- When a guarantor signs a guarantor's and you are likely to have to depend on the guarantor for repayment or obligation. Guarantors should not sign if they are not in willing to lend the money to the borrower themselves , since they make day in effect have to do just that .

13. See where the banks bank's money is going to be spent

14. Think first for your bank/NBFC , risk increases when credit principle violated. Good judgment, experience and common sense are the many of the good lending officer. The principles set out here are not perfect but are at your peril. If in doubt, ask yourself: "Would I lend my own money.

ANNEXURE-1

CAUTION INDUSTRY/SEGMENT LIST

1. Politicians / any applicant with Political Links
2. Film Personalities/TV and Film industry (actors / artists / producers / directors) / Film Distributors
3. STD/PCO outlets
4. Finance companies/ Private Money Lenders
5. Journalists
6. Security / Police personnel
7. Bars / Gambling Business / Massage Parlours/Beauty parlours
8. Waste merchants
9. DSA's / Verification Agencies / Collection Agencies / Repossession Agencies
10. Cable Operators / Video library owners/ Video Parlour
11. Interior designers (Non architects! non qualified)
12. Manpower Consultants / Placement Agencies / labour contractors
13. Multi level / Network marketing business
14. Motor training schools
15. Defence equipment — manufacture, trader, dealer
16. Houses of worship, religious organization and charities
17. Trading in endangered species or ivory products
18. Transport Operators (with less than 10 trucks)

Glossary

Accrual accounting : An accounting system in which revenue is recog- nized during the period in which it is earned, and expenses are recog- nized during the period in which they are incurred, whether or not cash is received or disbursed.

Amortization : The process of paying off an amount gradually by spreading the payments over several years.

Annual general meeting This is the annual meeting at which the directors are required to present the annual report and accounts to shareholders.

Annual report The company's annual accounts, audit statements and narrative account of the year at hand. Presentations vary considerably.

Assets: Any item owned by a company or individual that can be given a monetary value and used if necessary to pay debts. There are many kinds of assets, described by terms like current assets and fixed assets.

Audit : An official examination and checking of a company's accounts by an independent accountant called an auditor, to certify that the accounts (as presented by the directors) comply with the law, and in their opinion give a true and fair view of the company's affairs.

Auditors: Accountants who certify that the company's accounts have been reviewed in accordance with FRS (Financial Reporting Standards for the UK – see below) and note the findings of their inquiry.

Authorized signatories Persons authorized to sign on behalf of the company borrowing the money. Specimen signatures are usually in a study material let provided by the company. It is the bank's (i.e. analyst's) responsibility to verify this: if the signatory is not authorized, the company does not have to pay the money back.

Borrower risk : Risks pertaining to the company, including management, profitability, non-performance, and bankruptcy: all factors relating to the borrower.

Bullet repayment : A loan whose interest is payable at intervals agreed in the loan agreement, and whose principal is repayable in a lump sum at final maturity. The source of repayment is usually a new facility that is put into place.

Capital intensive : Thus is a balance sheet where a relatively large pro- portion of the assets is in plant and equipment. This means there are large depreciation charges with a high level of fixed costs, resulting in volatile earnings.

Capitalization (of an expenditure): This occurs when an expenditure is recorded as an asset, which is then written off over future periods. The justification for this is that the expenditure turned asset produces benefits beyond the calculated accounting period.

Certificates of registration : These certify that the company has regis- tered with the state authorities. Photocopies are usually available from the company on request.

Collateral: See Security.

Comparability: This is the concept that company accounts and their ratios are comparable, since companies are required to report them in a similar fashion.

Consolidated accounts : In a case where a parent company has a control- ling interet in other companies, that is, its subsidiaries, then the par- ent company must prepare consolidated or group accounts. Since the early 1900s US and UK companies have been required to publish group accounts. Seventh Directive on European harmonization focused on group accounts, and since 1990 they have been mandatory for all European companies. In the UK, companies which are required to pro- vide a consolidated balance sheet, must also provide one for the parent company that is called the company balance sheet. In the US, however, companies, which report on a consolidated basis, are not required to provide a parent company balance sheet.

Contingent liabilities: Items that do not represent a liability on the bal- ance sheet at the time of statement date but which could do so in the future. Such items include guarantees issued in favour of third parties, and lawsuits currently in progress whose outcome is uncertain.

Covenants: Conditions in the loan agreement signed by the bank and the borrower which the borrower must respect. Covenants can cover conditions on management performance, disposal of subsidiaries, negative pledges, amounts of debt incurred, and adherence to financial ratios. Non-compliance is known as an event of default.

Credit scoring : Technique used to evaluate a potential borrower according to a pre-defined matrix procedure. Usually used in retail banking and credit card processing, may be used in evaluating corporate.

Debenture : A debenture is a loan secured on the company's assets, normally with an agreed rate of interest and fixed repayment date.

Documentation : Anything (such as certificates of registration, loan agreements, guarantees, etc.) relating to the legal agreements and guarantees governing the facility extended to the borrower.

Documentation risk : The risk of non-repayment due to a defect in the loan agreement or security arrangements. This can arise due to faulty drafting, mitigating circumstances, juridically non-enforceable and faulty collateral, or guarantees which have expired and not been renewed. The analyst is not expected to assess legal issues, but is expected to obtain legal opinions when necessary and note them in the credit analysis.

Double entry study material keeping : Luca Pacioli authored the first study material on the double entry study material keeping entitled *De Computis et Scripturis* in 1494. This included details of the mechanics of double entry study material keeping (debits, or left hand entries in the study materials of account, and credits, or right hand entries). Thus, any amount is entered on the right hand side (credit) of one account and the same amount is entered on the left hand side (debit) of another account. This guarantees that at the end of the financial year it is possible to produce an income statement (in the UK called the profit and loss account), disclosing the profit or loss for the year and a balance sheet with assets (debit balances) equalling liabilities (credit balances).

DTI Department of Trade and Industry. It is a valuable source of infor- mation on companies and many business matters in the UK and abroad.

EBIT Earnings before deduction of interest expense and income taxes.

EBITDA Earnings before deduction of interest expense, income taxes, depreciation and amortization.

Equity : In the context of credit analysis, this refers to the net value of all assets after deduction of all charges. Also known as share capital or shareholders' funds.

Events of default : A pledge in the loan agreement which the borrower fails to meet, enabling the bank to call the loan in for prepayment. Such events can range from the Channel Tunnel boring failing to reach mile 12.75 on 25 October, to mailing an annual report 3 days late to the lending bank.

Evergreen facility : A facility that automatically renews itself unless the borrower or lender gives notice to cancel.

Factoring : Selling of invoices to raise cash. Debts of various kinds are put together and sold to banks or corporate treasurers. A term used in international trade.

FASB : This is the Financial Accounting Standards Board, which is the rule making body for the accounting profession in the US. Its mem- bers are appointed by a foundation, the members of which are selected by the directors of the American Institute of Certified Public Accountants.

Financial year end: The close of the year accounts, abbreviated as FYE.

Fiscal year end: The end of the tax year as defined by the tax authorities.

Fourth Directive : The Fourth Directive was adopted in 1978 and dealt with accounting principles, accounts and allied information with standard formats enforced for the income statement and balance sheet. It also contained the true and fair view requirement in the preparation of financial statements.

FRS/SSAP : Financial Reporting Standard/Statement of Standard Accounting Practices. A set of standardized guidelines and procedures which have become mandatory for directors in the UK for all company accounts.

Futures : These are formal agreements to purchase a given item in the future at a price agreed today. The purpose is to hedge against price changes. The practice began in Chicago in the 19th century and centred around the agricultural market, but records show that it was common in Holland and Japan in the 16th century.

GAAP : Generally Accepted Account Principles are rules that govern the preparation of financial statements, based on pronouncements of authoritative accounting organizations such as the Financial Accounting Standards Board, industry standards and accounting literature.

Gearing : This is a ratio that sums up the financial standing of a com- pany. It is obtained by dividing the total interest bearing debt by the shareholders' funds. The higher the number, the greater the risk. A com- pany that has a large proportion of its permanent capital from debt is referred to as being highly geared.

Guarantees: Usually an undertaking by a third party to assume the debts of the borrower in the event of default. A common situation with parent/affiliate lending arrangements. Guarantees can and do expire, and the analyst should ensure in the credit review that they are either still valid, or have been renewed.

Intangible assets Items which are valuable to a company but have no material form. These are trademarks, reputation, brand loyalty and copyrights, for example.

Investor/Creditor community: Entities which provide funds to companies.

Investors buy shares in the company (equity), while creditors lend money to companies (debt).

Lawsuits : Items which do not appear on the balance sheet but can have a financial impact on the company. Also considered as 'contingent liabilities', these should be explained in the notes to the financial statements.

Lending risk : The risks the bank is getting into by putting the loan into place. Often more narrowly defined as risk arising from inadequate or faulty loan documentation.

Leverage (1) This is the American term for gearing. (2) In the UK this is the same as gearing, with the addition of non-interest bearing external debt.

Liquidation: Selling off the company's assets to satisfy creditors during a winding up. The main risk in a liquidation is asset shrinkage : whether the assets being liquidated can fetch a market value sufficient to satisfy all the creditors.

Loan agreement Every loan should have one. These define the rules and obligations binding on the lenders, borrowers guarantors and related parties.

Loan officers : The persons who look after client relations and new busi- ness opportunities. The analyst's work is to evaluate objectively the companies and businesses loan officers are proposing to lend to, and submit their evaluations in the credit review process.

Loans, short-term Loans under one-year duration.

Loans, term : Loans of between 2 and 7 years' duration.

Market capitalization : This is the aggregate market value of all out- standing shares of a corporation.

Maturity schedules: The repayment dates on the loan. A good set of company financial statements will break out all the various debt which it has, the interest rates, and periods of repayment. The analyst should pay particular attention to the impact of bullet repayments on future cash flow.

Minority interests: If a company is not 100% owned by a parent com- pany, then the minority interest (the proportion of the subsidiary owned by those other than the parent company) is stated separately in the accounting statements. In order to help alleviate confusion (that is, double counting of profits), all intro group trading is eliminated, so that only revenue from dealing with customers outside the group of companies is shown in the income statement. Note that the minority interests are required to be credited with their proportion of any profit coming from intro group trading.

Plc : Public Limited Company. The term 'public' in plc refers to the size of the share capital of the company, so a plc does not necessarily have its shares quoted on the stock exchange. The public companies normally provide a preliminary outline statement on the year's financial performance within 3 months of the end of the company's financial year. The formal publication of the annual report follows thereafter.

Ratio analysis : The technique of analysing company performance by calculating financial ratios for historical and comparative purposes.

Regulatory actions   Legal requirements on a company. If the government passes a law forcing chemical companies to process carcinogenic waste instead of dumping it in our drinking water, this is known as a regulatory action. Regulatory issues can adversely impact a company's profitability and viability.

ROCE   Return on capital employed.

Security : The assets or guarantees you claim when the loan is in default.

Forms of security can vary from high-grade government bonds to par- tially completed stock, and are defined in the loan agreement.

Seventh Directive : The Seventh Directive was adopted in 1983 and was concerned with publicly quoted companies and the presentation of consolidated or group accounts, including the accounting treatment of goodwill.

Spreadsheet : The analyst's main tool in unscrambling a typical set of company accounts.

Subsidiaries : The annual report should provide details of all subsidiaries.

This includes the name, business, geographic location and the propor- tion of voting and other shares owned by the parent company. Where the subsidiary has been sold (or otherwise disposed of), these details should be reported as part of the notes on discontinued operations. This means that revenue and profit are then shown separately, and the profit or loss on disposal treated as an exceptional item in the income statement.

TNW   Total net worth.

Working capital : This is the current assets minus current liabilities and is used as an indicator of liquidity.

Yield : Usually expressed as a percentage, this represents the return earned from an investment.